P9-ELO-422

WHITETAIL STRATEGIES, VOL. II

WHITETAIL STRATEGIES, VOL. II

Straightforward Tactics for Tracking, Calling, the Rut, and Much More

PETER J. FIDUCCIA

THE LYONS PRESS
Guilford, Connecticut
An imprint of The Globe Pequot Press

The Lyons Press is an imprint of The Globe Pequot Press.

Printed in the United States of America

10 9 8 7 6 5 4 3 2 1

Library of Congress Cataloging-in-Publication Data

Fiduccia, Peter.
    Whitetail strategies. Vol. II : straightforward tactics on tracking,
    moon phase, calling, the rut, and much more / Peter J. Fiduccia.
       p. cm.
    ISBN 1-58574-852-8 (trade cloth)
    1. White-tailed deer hunting. I. Title.
    SK301.F5274 2005
    799.2'7652—dc22
                                                        2005002250

To my son, my best friend, and my hunting partner, P. Cody Fiduccia. You have enabled me to experience the unbridled exhilaration of having you share my love for deer hunting with your genuine interest and enthusiasm in the deer woods. The memories we've shared will last our lifetimes.

And to my three other deer hunting compadres: my wife, Kate, and my two cousins, Leo and Ralph Somma. Thanks for all the laughter and deer hunting prowess we shared over the last 35 years. I hope our children know the enjoyment of having the same wonderful camaraderie in the deer woods too.

CONTENTS

ACKNOWLEDGMENTS

I wanted to be a hunter for as long as I can remember. While most of my classmates at Fort Hamilton High School in Brooklyn, New York, were paying attention during classes, I occasionally drifted off in daydreams about hunting game.

I didn't know why I wanted to hunt. No one in my immediate or extended Italian family hunted. (I found out many years later that my mother's biological father was an avid hunter who had traveled the world hunting every kind of big game animal.) Whatever the reason, all I understood at the time was that I had a burning desire to hunt game.

I was seventeen years old when I was finally able to pursue my dream. I bought a deer tag and planned my first hunt in the small hamlet of Cranberry Lake in New York's Adirondack Mountains. Several of my friends and I rented a station wagon and lit out on our first big game safari. Many more were to follow.

Throughout college I continued to hunt a variety of game, particularly white-tailed deer, my favorite animal. Along with the hunts, I dreamed of being a well-known outdoor writer, like the ones whose articles I regularly read in *Field & Stream*, *Sports Afield*, and *Outdoor Life*, at that time the only "real" outdoor publications that carried hunting features.

A hard dose of reality set in when I began to work for a living. I had little time to daydream then. My job was the top priority. But I always made sure I took at least three weeks of vacation during the deer season. In the twenty years following my first deer hunting trip in 1964, I told anyone who would listen about my dream. The veteran deer hunters in a hunting club called the Ridge Runners, whose camp was in Hancock, New York, along NY 97, always lent an ear. I told them that someday I would write a book and magazine articles about the skills and tactics of being a successful deer hunter.

At the time, I was less than what one might refer to as a deer hunting expert. Put more accurately, I was a beginner. My hunting companions, however, were courteous and allowed me to take photos of them with their bucks, help track their wounded game, and ask hundreds of what I'm sure they thought were ridiculous questions. In their unwavering patience, they allowed me to "learn" how to field dress their deer and drag them to camp. Each and every member took his or her turn at that!

Later on, I met my soul mate, Kate Beekman. It didn't take me long to talk her ear off about deer hunting and my skills and knowledge. To my amazement, she not only listened politely, but also encouraged me to actually write an article about rattling for deer. Her support and strength were what finally took me from talking about writing to actually doing it.

I sent the article to the *New York Sportsman* magazine. I was shocked when Editor-in-Chief Paul Kessler wrote back to tell me the piece was "interesting and timely" and that he would pay me thirty dollars for it. That article launched my writing career. I owe Paul special thanks for taking a chance on a totally unknown and unproven outdoor writer.

Other thanks go to all the editors who accepted and published my articles over the next few years, including Lamar Underwood, Rick Sapp, Jay Cassell, and Gerry Bethge. Without their support and guidance, I would never have had the opportunity to do what I now do for a living. I'm grateful to all of them for helping me achieve my dream.

I also want to let every person who has read my books, magazine articles, and newspaper columns or watched my television programs or come to hear me speak at seminars all across the country that I have appreciated the support. I extend my deepest gratitude to all of you. Truth be known, without each and every one of you I wouldn't be able to make my living writing about hunting.

INTRODUCTION

As I do most deer seasons, I drove to upstate New York last year and hunted with my long-time business associate and friend, Peter Fiduccia, for a weekend. When I got to the farm—a 310-acre spread southeast of Syracuse—there was snow on the ground and the temperature was in the teens. Peter's cousin and long-time hunting partner, Leo Somma, who also owns 110 acres of the property, was at the house too. The plan was to get up at 4:30 A.M., have a quick breakfast, then head out to stands overlooking some well-used deer trails leading out of the fields into thick cover. I got to my blind well before light, and settled in for a morning of watching a number of deer runs that criss-crossed in front of me; behind me was a thick cedar swamp, while out in front of me, sixty yards away, was the edge of a sprawling cornfield. Five does ambled by at 8 o'clock, but that was all I saw in the early morning. Peter and Leo didn't see much either—which was surprising, as we all thought the single-digit early morning temperatures would get the deer moving.

The late-morning hunt was different. The temperature had risen into the teens—a warm spell!—and a front was supposed to come in later in the day. I headed to a different stand, one that overlooked a thicket of mixed hardwoods. Leo was up above on a ridge, while Peter was situated in a hemlock grove half a mile to the south. The plan was to stay in the stands until about 11 A.M., then Peter was going to get out of his stand and slowly stalk from his location into the area where Leo and I were located. At 11:15, I was watching in the direction from which Peter and any deer he might move toward me would be coming, when I heard a single shot, then quiet. A few minutes later, my Motorola radio crackled with Peter's voice; "Hey guys, I've got an eight-pointer down—can you come and help me out?"

Climbing out of the blind, I headed up the ridge, met up with Leo, and hiked over to the pine thicket from where Peter had called us . . . and, sure enough, there he was, with a beautiful eight-pointer on the ground, dead with a slug shot to the neck.

"I came out of my stand, and drove toward the lower forty to try to move some deer to you guys," Peter told us. "When I parked the ATV I noticed fresh tracks in the snow. One set of deer prints was large, so I thought I would follow it for awhile. I hadn't gone thirty yards from where I first cut the tracks when I saw a doe looking back at me, about sixty yards away. I quickly scanned for another deer and I spotted antlers moving next to her. They turned and slowly headed away. I quickly dropped down the trail and hiked over to a crossing where I suspected they were heading."

And that's exactly where those two deer went. The two deer eventually took the trail and went to the crossing where Peter was waiting for them. One shot, and his season was done.

Leo was laughing as Peter told the story. "Unbelievable," he said. "This stuff only happens to Peter. He gets out of his stand, drives to a spot to move some deer to us, and instead picks up the tracks of a buck and doe, and then he figures out how to ambush them after they see him, and winds up shooting the buck! Now you know why I don't let him push deer for me!"

We laughed about that as we walked back to the farmhouse, got the E-Z-Go, and drove back to pick up the eight-pointer. What luck . . .

But you know what? That wasn't luck, because over the twenty years that I have hunted with Peter, I've seen him do this many times before. I remember a hunt with him in Texas a number of years ago. I shot a respectable ten-pointer on the ranch on the third day of the hunt, while our friend Dan took a heavy-beamed 125-class buck the next day. During the hunt, despite seeing several good bucks, Peter didn't shoot anything—at least, not until the last day of the hunt. After lunch that last day, he announced that he wanted to try hunting an out-of-the-way stand near which he had seen some good buck sign on the first day of the hunt. "I've just got a good feeling about that spot," he told us.

At dusk, he came back with a 155-inch ten-point buck, a real Texas trophy.

Then there was the time a few years ago when he was hunting in his hometown of Warwick, New York. He and I had put up some stands earlier in the year, and when we finished putting up the second stand Peter announced confidently, "One or both of us are going to shoot really good bucks from one of these stands. They're situated in the perfect spots for mature bucks to use— especially during the late season." We hunted them a few times, then work overwhelmed us both and neither one of us had a chance to hunt them again for the rest of the regular firearms season. When blackpowder season rolled around in mid-December, Peter called and said, "Let's hunt our hotspot on the mountain," but I was too swamped with work to get out and didn't go.

So was Peter. But I remember talking with him on the phone on a Thursday, right around lunchtime. Peter said he shouldn't do it, but he just had to get out and hunt that area at least one afternoon before the season closed. That night I got an e-mail: Peter had found the tracks of a big buck in a new snowfall and had followed them until it started to get dark.

Returning to the same area the next day, Peter picked up the tracks of the deer again, but when he caught up to the cagey buck, it reacted quicker than Peter did and gave him the slip. On the third day—work was obviously of secondary importance at this point—you guessed it, he found and shot a monster buck with a huge twelve-point rack that was high and had a lot of mass.

"I thought about how that buck slipped away twice, and came up with a game plan that I thought would work. I took the long way in to the area and set up on a ledge across from where I thought the buck was bedding during the day," Peter's e-mail read. "I set up my decoy natural deer tail and started jigging it as I made several soft grunts. Within minutes I saw only the buck's antlers as he sneaked in below me to check out the tail and the estrus doe blat sounds coming from it. The buck was staring at the tail as I placed the scope on his chest and let the .50 caliber sabot fly. The illusion of a hot doe flicking her tail in brush was what it took for this buck to drop his guard." (There's a photo of that buck on page 38, by the way.) As Peter dragged the buck out one of the buck's antlers pulled free. Because the buck's body was unusually thin, Peter aged the buck's teeth and discovered it was 10½ years old. The buck's advanced age accounted for his thin frame and for this antler falling off so early.

I could go on and on about Peter's successes, but I'll let you read the book, and relive those hunts with him. The point, though, is that this man really does have a special knack, a talent, for being where the bucks are. This doesn't come through luck, because it happens way too many times for that.

No, it happens because he knows how to look at terrain and figure out where the deer—especially mature bucks—are likely to be. From a career of reading sign, calling, rattling, using unusual decoys, following tracks, listening to and observing deer in a variety of habitats, he has got this buck-hunting game figured out better than most. As you read this book, you'll see that for yourself. Peter Fiduccia is the real deal—he knows his stuff, and now he's letting you in on a lifetime's worth of knowledge. Read the book, study it, be adaptable. Go with your instincts. If your gut tells you that this area doesn't hold deer, go with it; move to another area. And if your instincts tell you that a buck is in the area, read the signs and interpret them! Then put your deer hunting skills to the test.

It's all about knowing your quarry, and having confidence in your knowledge. Then your instincts are going to be right, more often than not. As *Field & Stream* editor Sid Evans notes on this book's cover, if Peter Fiduccia knew any more about deer, he would be a deer. You can attain that level, too, and this book will help you do it faster than any other deer hunting book I know.

Jay Cassell
Katonah, New York
March, 2005

Tracking

Ted Rose

Chapter

1

DEFINING TRACKING

The ability to follow tracks left by a deer until you actually catch sight of the animal is a crucial element in becoming a more skillful hunter.

There are two types of tracking. The first is an absolute necessity for any dedicated, ethical deer hunter. This is the ability to track a wounded animal by the blood trail or by "sign" left on the forest floor, grass, branches, vegetation, and even rocks along its escape route. This type of tracking ends when the hunter finds the dead deer or is able to spot it and finish it off.

This is a tracking skill that every hunter must learn in order to lessen the chance of losing a wounded deer. Odds are, whether you're a seasoned veteran or a novice, sometime during your hunting life you will wound a deer and have to follow its blood trail in order to recover it. Despite what your friends or other hunters may say, the wounding of one, and sometimes even a few, deer over a lifetime of hunting is inevitable, no matter how fine a shot you are. Following up on wounded game has been part of the hunt since our caveman ancestors first began hurling spears. As hunters, we all have a moral responsibility to recover a wounded deer. And that recovery starts with understanding how to effectively follow tracks, blood, and other sign.

To become proficient at this type of tracking takes practice, persistence, and patience. For better or worse, the more trails of wounded deer you follow, the better you will become at finding injured game. Every blood trail is unique, but the information gained with each experience can be applied to all future tracking endeavors. Those who pay attention will learn something new on each outing.

The second type of tracking is more romantic. It conjures up that spark for adventure lying deep in every hunter. The ability to find the track of a deer on the hoof and follow it until you're able to get a clean shot at the animal, especially a mature buck, is to most hunters the ultimate deer hunting experience.

To be skilled enough to trail a buck by following his tracks and finally tagging him on *his* turf, while playing by *his* rules, is the epitome of sport. For most of us, it generates a feeling of satisfaction like no other hunting tactic. To this day, when I daydream about taking a wise old buck with a heavy, wide set of antlers, a long drop tine, and a few gnarly kickers, I imagine that I cross his track while I'm slowly still-hunting through the woods after a fresh snowfall.

Of course, in my mind's eye the track is wide, long, and set deep in the snow. The distance between each hoof print is unusually long. And there is always some defect in the hoof to set the track apart from that of other bucks—lest I confuse it as I set out to walk him down. My dream takes me over mountains, through swamps, into thickets and cedar forests, and eventually back the other way as the buck tries to circle behind me.

Just before the end of legal shooting light, I spot him as he stops to check his back trail. Without the deer ever seeing me, I send a brush-cutting .44 caliber bullet whistling over the blowdowns. Before the big buck can react to the report of the rifle, the bullet finds its mark and the animal drops instantly and quietly into the fresh snow.

I've had this daydream many times during my hunting life, and I'll bet most of you've had some version of it, too.

While almost all whitetail hunters like to fantasize about duplicating the efforts of the well-known trackers of Maine and Vermont—like Hal Blood, the Benoits, and the Berniers—grandiose ideas about this tactic must be tempered with heavy doses of reality and common sense.

The most overlooked truth about tracking by most buck hunters across the nation, especially those in heavily hunted areas, is that in order to become the next Blood, Benoit, or Bernier (I often quip that perhaps to be a famous tracker from New England, your last name must begin with the letter "B") a hunter must have unpressured hunting territory, and plenty of it. This is the single most important element for tracking down bucks as consistently as the legendary trackers mentioned above.

A successful tracker must also know how to quickly interpret track sign left by deer. Orienteering skills must be honed carefully. And when trailing bucks in big woods, the tracker must be in good physical shape. I often compare this type of deer hunting to hunting sheep because following a buck up and down ridges, over blowdowns, and through thickets, swamps, and bogs can quickly sap the strength of even the most athletic hunter, especially in the legs.

Successful tracking in the wild backcountry of Maine, or in remote regions throughout New England, the upper Midwest, the southern Appalachians, and Canada, requires a lot of patience; more patience than most hunters possess. Perhaps even more important is unwavering persistence. Without this attribute, you are better off never taking up the track of a buck in big woods country.

Legendary guide Hal Blood has the strength and endurance necessary to track long hours up and down Maine's mountains and through its swamps and lowlands. (Debbie Blood)

But these elements are not all that make up a skilled tracker. It's just as important for a hunter to know when to give up on the track. We've all read about trackers following prints overnight and into the next morning. And although that sounds exciting and adventurous, it really isn't practical. The fact is, in most states, such activity is actually considered illegal. Even without a firearm, following a buck during the night constitutes "harassment of wildlife" for most game departments. Chasing after a buck at night is essentially hunting, and as far as I know, hunting at night is prohibited in every state.

If the buck isn't located and killed by legal sunset, the ethical sportsman should understand that he has lost the battle of the chase for the day. Anything less pushes the ethical edges of hunting and fair chase. Dogging a buck overnight—even with only a flashlight stowed away in your backpack—will test the patience of almost any game warden.

Posted signs act as a reality check for hunters in places other than the big woods.

Any story about tracking a buck overnight and staying with the track until shooting light the next morning is, in my view, a vast exaggeration of the truth. Staying with a deer through the dead of night, over hill and dale, and running him ragged until you spot him the next morning, and then shooting him, and then still being in good enough shape to drag out this 300-pound buck . . . well, it's just a bunch of hooey. It's meant to sell magazines and to make other trackers feel less confident in their own skills. But anyone can track a deer at night. There's no magic involved, as the deer is less spooky about what's on his back trail.

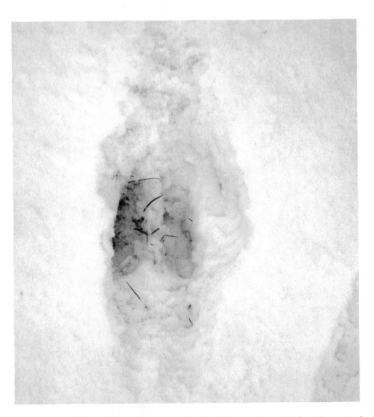

I estimated that this track was made less than an hour before I spotted it. I saw the buck two hours later, and although his body was big, his antlers were not. I decided to pass on him.

This has been proven time and again when hunters are walking out of the woods after leaving their stands once legal shooting hours are over. During the egress, many of us have bumped into a buck or doe. Instead of snorting and immediately running away, these deer often remain frozen in their tracks trying to "make you

I had followed this buck's tracks for about thirty minutes when I heard a shot ring out ahead of me. The lucky hunter told me the deer was checking its back trail when he dropped it.

out." I've had mature bucks walk within feet of me when trying to identify what I was, even as the wind was blowing my scent directly to them. A lot of other hunters have had the same experience. Darkness just seems to make deer less afraid of human scent and/or human outlines than daylight. So dogging a buck at night isn't necessarily the challenge it has been hyped up to be.

The fact is, the longer you track a buck, the greater the chances that another hunter will shoot him. I can't tell you how many times I've taken up the trail of a buck in the snow in country that is under-hunted, only to hear the report of a firearm up ahead. In most cases, I followed the track until it led me to the dead buck and the hunter who shot him. My conversation with the successful hunter usually reveals that he shot the buck as it was "checking its back trail."

I share these negatives not to discourage you from becoming a tracker, but rather to give you confidence and to offer some common sense about the tactic.

KNOW YOUR TERRAIN

If you have ever hunted deer in Maine, you've learned a few things about just how wild that state can be. Most of Maine is a maze of thick wilderness. Even its systems of logging roads can be confusing to the first-time hunter.

Several years ago while bear hunting there, I drove my truck into the hunting area by following my outfitter, who was driving ahead of me. He directed me to my stand and told me to "just reverse the directions and you'll find your way out without any trouble." I have a great sense of direction, so I didn't think twice about it as I headed to my stand. I had even noted each turn on the many logging roads on a tape recorder as we traveled in. Just before the outfitter left, he asked, "Do you think you'll be able to find your way back?" I smiled with confidence, "Of course."

By now you've probably surmised that when I tried to drive out in the pitch dark, all the logging roads looked the same. It was hard to differentiate the landmarks I had recorded earlier. Each turn left me feeling like I'd made a mistake. Nothing looked familiar in the dark.

I became hopelessly lost. So lost that after four hours of trying in vain to find my way back to the main road, I had to radio for help. Not that I wasn't calling in earlier—I was. But I couldn't raise the base camp. Finally, I reached a highpoint on a small knoll where the radio worked. After I told them what had happened, I could hear the howls of laughter from the other hunters in camp, including my guest, former baseball great Wade Boggs.

Over the radio, the outfitter told me, "Stop where you are and don't move again. When you see my lights, beep your horn and call me on the radio." It took him—and several other hunters who came along to see the hunter who was lost in his truck—over an hour to locate me. When they finally did, I wasn't the least bit embarrassed or ashamed of getting lost.

This was big country, very big, and it all looked exactly the same. Unless a person is very familiar with traveling the network of logging roads in the backcountry, getting lost, even in daylight, is all too easy.

The same holds true when hunting through any big woods you're unfamiliar with. Before you set out on the track of a deer in strange country, you'd better think twice—no, make that three times. You must have years of experience with the land you hunt before attempting to track a buck (or in my case, drive a truck) for miles and miles.

When you're tracking a buck in the snow, it's easy to become a little too confident that you can retrace your footsteps to get out. Even in snow, retracing your steps can be problematic. Moreover, an unexpected snowstorm, wind, or heavy rain can

When tracking bucks in areas like the remote wilderness country of New York's Adirondack Mountains, hunters need to remain aware of their surroundings and the amount of daylight left. (Ted Rose)

obliterate your back trail, making it impossible to follow your tracks back out of the woods.

I learned that lesson early in my deer hunting career, forty years ago when I was just seventeen. It was my first hunt in the Adirondack Mountains of New York—a vast wilderness that in places compares to anything Maine can offer. I was hunting in the town of Childwold, on a 50,000-acre tree farm owned by

International Paper. It was the fourth day of the hunt. On the way to my stand that afternoon, which was about five hundred yards from a logging road and about a thousand yards from where I had parked my truck, I cut a big track in the fresh snow. (Back in those days it still snowed in October in northern New York.)

Thinking I had learned enough about the area to follow the track, I took off after the deer. It was 2:30 PM when I began tracking, my first mistake. I walked slowly and slightly off to the side of the track, cutting back to it every so often to check that it was the same print. After an hour or so, I spotted the buck. I still remember his rack. It was probably smaller than I picture it today, but he was the first buck I had ever tracked in the "big" woods, and his image is permanently etched in my mind.

As I slowly raised my rifle, he casually disappeared into a heavy stand of pine trees. I followed him in. The evergreens were immense, and the buck led me on a wild goose chase as he continually circled around me. I spotted him two more times—each time for only a moment. The last time I saw him, I suddenly realized how dark it was getting. I could hardly see him in the scope. I glanced at my watch; it was 4:20. Fear instantly overtook me, another mistake.

I knew I had to immediately abandon the track and try to get back to my vehicle. But I didn't find my way out that day. As the light faded, even following my back trail became difficult. I spent the most harrowing night of my young life hopelessly lost in the Adirondacks. I walked and walked and called and called for help. (I didn't understand back then that I should have remained where I was.) No one answered. I shot most of my shells, keeping only a few in case I met up with a bear in a foul mood.

By dawn I was tired, scared, hungry, wet, disoriented, and about to freak out when I heard voices. I ran toward them, and to my joy and shock I emerged on a trail that Boy Scouts—yes, little

This buck was being tracked on a 1,000-acre farm when it was inadvertently pushed toward another hunter. Knowing when to back off a track helps prevent this problem.

Boy Scouts—were happily walking along. The scoutmaster quickly scolded me for carrying a firearm on Boy Scout property. It didn't take him long, after sizing me up, to realize that my story about getting lost was true.

It turned out that I had walked miles from my truck overnight—many miles. The scout leader took me to camp, warmed me up, fed me, calmed me down, and drove me back to my vehicle. I won't tell you how far.

The lesson I learned, and the one I'd like to share with anyone who wants to track deer, is to know your hunting area as well as you know your own backyard before you step one foot down that trail.

All that aside, tracking down and bagging a buck can be the most challenging and satisfying of all deer hunting tactics. Only a conditioned hunter with experience, skill, and knowledge can become a seasoned, consistently successful deerstalker. Once mastered, however, the art of stalking a buck can bag you deer when other hunters can't seem to tag out.

Ted Rose

Chapter

2

REAL-WORLD TRACKING

During my long hunting career, I've tracked many elk, moose, mule deer, white-tailed deer, and an even a few bear. Aside from whitetails, I have only successfully tracked and shot two bull elk out of that group of animals. But when it comes to tracking deer, I've had much better success. Through the years I've tried to get the drop on seventy-five whitetails by following their tracks. Now that may not seem like a lot of deer tracking. But for my type of hunting, and for the areas I hunt, it is.

Although some hunters, like the famous trackers of New England, hunt bucks almost exclusively by tracking them, in real-world deer hunting the majority of hunters track deer only incidentally to the more common tactics. Real-world conditions mean hunting in smaller woodland areas with some degree of hunting pressure. It just isn't possible in most cases to trail bucks over long distances due to private lands and the number of other hunters in the woods. Most hunters pick up what appears to be a big fresh buck track in the snow while on the way to their stands, during a deer drive, or when slowly still-hunting through the woods hoping to spot or jump a deer from cover.

This is how I generally decide to follow a deer track, too. It is rare that I leave camp with the sole intention of riding along a logging road or walking down a trail looking for a buck track. And it is very rare for me to pass up what looks like a good track to continue searching for an ever larger track, like so many of the more famous trackers say they do. So, I guess I'm a casual tracker in comparison to some hunters, or perhaps more accurately, an incidental one. I track, but only when the spirit or sign moves me to. For my type of hunting, it works perfectly.

Even though I've taken up the track of seventy-five deer, I can count the number of successful hunts—where following the trail ended up with me actually killing a buck—on one hand and the finger of another.

I caught one off-guard while he was feeding on the branch of a cedar tree. Another buck met his fate when I noticed his prints were getting closer together in the snow, suggesting that he was slowing down. I shot him as he tried to sneak away by unhurriedly walking up a small creek. I shot my last tracked buck after I spotted him trying to circle downwind to see what was dogging him. I quickly but quietly got to a location where I could cut him off. An interesting note here is that all the bucks were tracked in snow that was between three and six inches deep.

Each and every tracking experience, whether successful or not, taught me something and helped me become a better tracker in the heavily hunted areas and the type of terrain that I frequent. I believe I learned more from the numerous deer that eventually gave me the slip than I did from the bucks I was able to outsmart.

The best strategy for successful tracking in heavily pressured areas—or in wilderness areas, for that matter—is to know the travel routes of the deer. Know what to expect from a wise old buck that's used to having someone dogging his trail. Know what he'll do

This dandy twelve-point buck was taken in a remote area that I avoid hunting until late in the season. I prefer at least three inches of snow on the ground for tracking. (Kate Fiduccia)

under that type of pressure. What are his favorite escape trails? Where will he head when nervous about being followed? How will he react to your pressure? If you know these things in advance of your actual hunt, you can plan a tracking tactic that will work.

Even the best tracker stops to lay out a plan when he cuts a track. In some cases, he even sends for reinforcements. A call over the radio, where legal, brings a few other ardent trackers to-gether. The stalker with the most stamina is elected to take up the track. Before he does, where legal, the other two or three hunters plan to take up stands—sometimes a long distance away from the track, far enough away that the stalker must wait an hour or so before starting after the buck.

Just moments after tracking and shooting a doe, my wife, Kate, called on the radio to let me know where to meet her with the E-Z-Go. Radios should only be used for emergencies or to advise fellow hunters of downed deer.

Once in place, they signal each other and the tracking begins. The primary stalker gets on the track and stays with it until he jumps the buck and shoots it himself or until he pressures the buck enough that it becomes so worried about its back trail that it forgets to pay as much attention to what lies ahead. Often, the buck winds up walking into one of the hunters who has taken a stand on a known escape route or on a logging road that crosses from one section of property to another. This is, in fact, how most trackers get their bucks. It is a rewarding hunt, filled with challenges.

But this strategy is not for the unskilled, or for those who lack patience and persistence. It is especially not for those who don't know enough to call off the stalk in fairness to both the sport and the deer, if and when that time arrives. The ethics of hunting should always be uppermost in your mind.

A LESSON PASSED ON

A couple of years ago I was hunting a farm I had just purchased in the southern tier of New York. I was with my wife, Kate, and long-time hunting companions and twin cousins Leo and Ralph Somma. Opening day dawned with over eighteen inches of new snow, and more was still falling. Ralph called on the radio and asked me to meet him by his stand. When I got there, he told me he had shot a nice eight-point buck and wanted some help tracking it. I brought along Leo and my fourteen-year-old son, Cody.

Ralph suggested that since we didn't know the land well yet, he would take a stand where we suspected the buck might circle back. Meanwhile, I was going to pick up the track and blood trail and slowly follow after the deer.

I took my son along to give him experience tracking a wounded deer. We weren't on the track more than a hundred yards when I turned to Cody and whispered, "Judging by the tracks and the blood in the snow, this buck is slowing down. He should be close by." Those words had barely left my mouth when the buck jumped up from behind a deadfall not ten yards to my left. In the surprise and excitement of the moment, I fired and missed. The buck ran off in a different direction.

Rattling, calling, or using decoys eliminates the need to track deer. Jay Cassell likes to use real deer antlers, in conjunction with grunts and doe blats, to lure bucks into range.

Again, we picked up the track. This time, there was much less blood to help us. I could see from the hoof prints that the buck was about to bed down ahead of us. I told Cody to keep a sharp eye out. Fifty yards later, he spotted the buck sneaking off to our left through some heavy pines. The buck didn't offer us a shot, but he was heading in a direction that would soon put him in Ralph's path.

Each time we jumped the buck, the possibility of it being shot by another hunter on an adjoining property became more and more realistic, especially since it was opening day. With this in mind we slowed our pace, hoping that the buck would slow his as well. Just then, a single muffled report from Ralph's 12-gauge Browning Deer Stalker rang out not one hundred yards from us. I was able to show Cody that with a little patience, enough understanding to not pressure the buck, and a solid plan, it's possible to put together a good tracking effort.

This is real-world tracking. Like most hunters, I don't get the chance to track deer in remote wilderness areas like Maine or the Adirondacks on a regular basis. In fact, when I'm hunting with an outfitter while taping a segment for our TV show, *Woods N' Water*, we don't track a mature buck with me, the guide, and a cameraman, no matter how remote the area. Doing so would cut the odds of bagging a buck down to a percentage neither the guides nor I can accept. I only have a limited amount of time to produce the show, and we stand a better chance of scoring if I take a stand, rattle, or call.

All the bucks I've tracked and shot were in areas where other hunters were present. In my view, that is just as much of an achievement as picking up the track of a wilderness buck and taking it to the final confrontation. In fact, I believe it actually requires more hunting and tracking skills than wilderness tracking. But in the end both types are challenging and require specialized hunting skills, equipment, and tactics for success.

PLAY THE ODDS

When I cut a track and follow it, I manage to eventually see the buck about 70 percent of the time. This is a testament to how successful tracking can be under the right circumstances. The other 30 percent of the bucks I've tracked were never spotted, and I wasn't able to tell if anyone else shot at or killed them. I simply never caught up with those phantoms. They eluded all my attempts at running them down and won the match by giving me — and the other hunters around them — the slip.

Even though most of the bucks I've tracked and killed lived on lands that could be hunted by others, they were all taken in hard-to-reach places. This usually meant mountainous areas that I considered under-hunted, tough terrain where most hunters don't like to go. These areas are high and steep, and once a hunter expends the effort to get up there and that far back in, there is usually very little hunting pressure with which to contend.

Only one of the bucks I tracked successfully was taken in big woods wilderness country. In fact, several of the bucks were shot in southern Orange County, within fifty miles of Manhattan, New York. I attribute my success in catching up with all of these bucks, however, almost solely to the element of low hunting pressure.

Consistently successful tracking goes hand-in-hand with unpressured hunting grounds. Don't let anyone ever tell you anything different about tracking. But these types of areas can be found anywhere you hunt, no matter how populated the area is. You can always find some type of terrain that other hunters aren't willing to enter, such as swamps, steep mountains, and other forbidding areas. Hunt these areas, and your chances of catching up to a buck whose tracks you're following will increase tenfold.

HOOF TRACKS

There are, of course, other elements that help make a tracker more successful. First and foremost, an overwhelming majority of successful tracking is done in fresh, soft snow that isn't too deep.

Make it your business to learn all you can about a deer's hoof prints. For instance, I don't believe the length of a track is as

Kate pauses to determine whether she should follow the tracks. The snow is perfect; fresh and not too deep or soft.

important as its width. If a track is 3 to 3½ inches wide, I know that I'm following a mature deer.

Only experience can help you judge the significance of a track's depth in mud, snow, or sand. A mature buck puts most of his weight on his front quarters when walking, so it's obvious that his front feet will sink deeper into the ground than his rear feet. If the track you're following has front prints that are deeper, you're most likely on a mature buck track.

Mature bucks swagger as they walk. This means that their front right and left tracks appear staggered, another indication you're following an older buck. Smaller bucks and does leave tracks that are much closer together.

One other fact: A whitetail's walking stride is about 18 to 19 inches, calculated at a steady pace of about 3½ to 4 miles per hour (which is just a little faster than the average human pace). Their

The overall length, splayed hoof, and deep dewclaws of this print indicate that its maker was probably a mature buck, but you should always check for other sign to confirm this. (Ted Rose)

trotting gait is 30 to 36 inches, which translates to a speed of about 10 to 12 mph.

Use the above guidelines and your own observations to assess how far apart the tracks are when the deer is walking, trotting, or running. And learn to detect the other factors that provide valuable information about whether the track you're looking at actually belongs to a buck or a mature, heavy doe. Remember, a mature buck acts differently, thinks differently, eats differently, and especially walks differently than other deer. Bucks walk in a random way, often stopping to make or freshen a rub or scrape. In snow cover,

A buck will usually urinate after he has finished rubbing. The fresh urine is clearly visible in snow cover—a sure sign the buck isn't far ahead. (Ted Rose)

you will see where a buck has urinated between his tracks. You'll discover that does, even mature does, usually leave almost perfect heart-shaped tracks. They also walk in a straight line.

A crucial element in tracking is to learn to identify the track as soon as you pick up the trail. Study the print to see what makes it different from other deer tracks in the area. Quickly burn its image into your mind. If your buck joins up with other deer, you must be able to single out its track to stay on the correct trail.

TRACK AGE

If you're tracking during a snowfall that suddenly stops and you find tracks that haven't filled with snow yet, your buck probably isn't very far ahead. In fact, depending on what the buck is doing, he may only be fifteen to thirty minutes in front of you. A fresh track is always more defined, too, especially around the edges. Older tracks show signs of crumbling around the edges and are less defined.

One very important aspect of this learning process is understanding which tracks are fresh enough to set out after and which aren't. Only experience can guide you. It took me a long time to develop this skill. I eventually learned to place my boot print next to the buck track and compare the two. If the deer track appears a lot less defined than my track, I typically estimate that it is too old to follow. If it is somewhat less sharp than the boot print, but reasonably close, it is usually worth stalking. If it is just as sharp as your boot print, then get on it quickly.

ESCAPE ROUTES

It bears repeating that you must know your hunting area well to track deer successfully. Even more important, you need to know where the deer escape routes are. This is especially true for the real-world type of tracking most of us do. Knowing an escape route for a wilderness buck is somewhat less important, simply because the buck has so many choices available to it when covering a lot of ground. Bucks with limited territory available are more inclined to quickly head toward an escape route than their big woods cousins. This simply means that a hunter who knows where these escape routes are greatly increases his chances when tracking bucks in heavily hunted areas.

Learn where deer want to go when they're being pressured by something on their back trail. Know as many escape routes as possible. Learn to anticipate what a buck being followed by a predator will and won't do, or where he'll head in good weather versus bad weather, on wet ground or in snow. Bucks have a sixth sense about snow. They instinctively know they are easier to follow in snow and react differently when pursued in it.

MIND AND BODY

Next come the essentials that separate the really good trackers from the casual ones. These are the elements of mind and body. A serious tracker has character. He or she is able to muster the spirit to go on when the body and mind want nothing more than to quit. This person has the ability to stay totally focused on the job at hand and is able to dig deep when everything else tells him to turn back. Good trackers have the competitive spirit. They want to succeed.

The buck shares this intense desire. Its instinct for survival tells it to put as much distance as possible between it and whatever is on its back trail.

One of the most impressive trackers in big woods country, Hal Blood, has all of the above qualifications. In the book *Hunting Big Woods Bucks*, Blood emphasizes his dogged approach to

Once a tracker like Hal Blood spots a nice buck print in the snow, his quarry is in real trouble. (Hal Blood)

following a track. He makes it clear that his tenacity for outlasting bitterly cold temperatures, deep snow, mountainous terrain, wind, and even rain overcomes any desire his body sends to his mind to quit the trail. Anyone who intends to track mature bucks in big woods must first commit to being a determined tracker like Hal Blood.

An example of a single-minded tracker in heavily pressured hunting areas, especially when on the track of a wounded buck in snow or on bare ground, is my hunting companion, Ralph Somma. His ability to focus on nothing else besides staying on the track and sign is incredible. I have seen many other hunters quit a trail over the years, only to have Ralph pick it up, follow the track, and find the animal. This type of concentration is absolutely imperative when you're trailing tracks or a blood trail in high-pressure areas where there are numerous other hunters.

Not many hunters have the dogged perseverance of my hunting companion Ralph Somma when it comes to tracking whitetails, especially wounded bucks. (Ralph Somma)

KNOW WHEN TO HOLD UP

There are times when you need to pick up the pace and move fast while tracking. Other times, it's much better to slow down to a snail's pace, almost like you're still-hunting. Watching a buck's tracks closely will reveal what he is doing and how you should proceed.

When you push too hard, you might see a flash of brown or glimpse the sun reflecting off an antler as the buck drifts into a patch of cover. Don't expect a mature buck to flag as it sneaks away. A wise old buck learns to tuck his tail between his legs, especially when he has a predator on his back trail. And that's what a tracker is to a buck, just another predator.

I mention this because it's a little-known fact that mature male game animals—like whitetail and muley bucks, bull elk, and moose—that live among predators learn to lead secretive lives. They instinctively know they should avoid being caught with a group or herd of their kin. They resign themselves to being loners. They have evolved with a sharp instinct to outmaneuver their pursuer rather than blindly run from danger. The older the animal, the more ingrained this behavior is in his psyche.

Therefore, the wise or seasoned tracker rarely expects to see a flagging, running buck as he tracks his prey. He knows that he is more likely to see a buck sneaking off ahead of him.

On the other hand, if you track too slowly you might never see the deer at all.

But if the tracking is done correctly, the reward will be a shot at your trophy. If the buck's tracks have a longer stride than they did earlier, he has picked up the pace. Once you figure this out, you must increase your speed, too. If his tracks begin to wander or he paces around nervously in a very small area or begins to circle, he's on to you and is preparing to give you the slip. This is the time to slow down and fine-tune your pursuit by keeping all your senses at full alert and moving one careful step at a time. Constantly scan the surrounding terrain, and proceed with extreme caution—he most probably isn't far away.

Learning what to do and when to do it will make you a better tracker. Again, experience is the best guide, so get in as much practice as possible.

Concentrate on looking at what is in front of you, but not directly in front of you. Most bucks that are being tracked have a habit, a natural instinct, to move off their track and watch for their pursuer's approach from one side or the other. Another problem is that too many first-time trackers, and even some who have been at it awhile, often become too intent on studying the tracks. This is one of the most common and costly mistakes a tracker can make. Keep your head up most of the time.

With bucks that slow up and hide to check out their back trail, it's possible for the hunter to actually see the deer several times during a stalk. This is part of what makes tracking so exciting.

LOOK HIGH AND LOW

Another tracking tip to remember is that bucks love to get higher than pursuers on their back trail, even if it's only slightly higher. On one occasion while hunting whitetails in Montana, we were following a track through a clearcut. The terrain was flat, but there were several piles of blowdowns and brush. The clearcut twisted and turned for over a mile in front of us. Each time we rounded a bend into a new clearing, I expected to see a buck sneaking off from behind a blowdown or brush pile.

Halfway through, I noticed that the buck's tracks were getting much closer together. He was milling about before moving off again. I realized he couldn't be too far ahead so I slowed my pace. As I scanned the blowdowns, a slight movement caught my attention. I saw the buck staring at me as he stood on the only bare rise in the entire clearcut. It was only two feet high and five feet wide, but it offered him what the blowdowns couldn't—a clear, unobstructed view of the predator on his back trail. Before I could react, he was gone. I logged the incident in my mind and have never forgotten it. I've seen mature bucks use this tactic to escape their pursuers many times since then.

This buck paused on a high spot in the terrain to check his back trail, a common trait among cagey deer. The wise tracker knows this and approaches such areas carefully. (Ted Rose)

So always pay close attention when you come to a knoll or even the slightest increase in elevation in the topography. If you do, you'll never get caught with your pants down. It is crucial to keep a keen eye on the natural cover off to the side and ahead of you. Glance from side to side, look for an antler, an eye, a nose, or even the entire deer.

You've probably read that it is better to look for parts of deer when still-hunting, but when you're tracking a deer you must be ready for anything. I can't tell you how many times I've been surprised, even shocked, to come around a bend or to enter a stand of pines only to see the buck just standing there looking back over his shoulder at me. Sometimes, I've come up on them while they were facing their back trail. This usually happens after they have been dogged for a longer period than they want to tolerate. Seasoned trackers always know to be alert to what may lie ahead when they're following a set of tracks.

UNIQUE TRACKS

Several years ago, just after a snow had stopped around 3:00 PM one day, I immediately went hunting on a ridge behind my old house. I found an unusual track with a well-defined chip in the left hoof. It led me to a ravine that I knew well. Most of the time, only young bucks occupied it. (I firmly believe that certain areas attract young bucks and other parts of the terrain attract mature bucks.) Even though the track was indicative of an older deer, I wasn't entirely convinced since I rarely saw big bucks in this area.

As I approached the ledge, a huge-racked buck sprung up from beneath me. Before I could get my Knight black-powder rifle up, he was gone. By that time it was already late and I decided not to give chase in hopes that he would return to this spot over the next couple of days.

The following day it snowed again. When the snow finally tapered off about ten o'clock in the morning, I left to go hunting. Once again, I picked up the chipped hoof tracks of the buck's trail heading in the same direction. I approached with extreme caution this time.

As I got to the deep ravine, I glanced at the tracks and saw that they meandered down between the rocks on the ledge toward the spot he had jumped up from the day before. I was looking hard at this spot when out of the corner of my eye I saw him just slightly above me and to my right. He had gone down the ledge, then doubled back up to bed at a high spot just off to the right. From this position, he could watch anything that came up from the valley below. Pretty cagey, huh? Again, he was gone before I had a chance to react.

But this time I had plenty of daylight left for following his tracks. I saw him twice over the next several hours. I was tired, however, and my reaction time was much slower than his. The buck had won the match yet again. I figured that the chances of his returning to this location would be slim to none. I headed home to get some rest, hoping I'd be able to cut his very unusual track again in the area where I broke off trailing him.

The next day I left at dawn. I took a different route to where I had stopped the hunt the day before. But as I began to climb the mountain, I again cut the fresh tracks of my buck. They were coming from the cornfields across the road. He too was heading up the mountain.

Making an educated guess that he was going to the spot where I had jumped him twice before, I alternately walked and trotted to beat him to it. I hoped the buck was taking his time, meandering and stopping to browse on his way up the mountain. When I reached the target area, I set up a deer-tail decoy for insurance. If I was successful in cutting the buck off, I intended to distract him by twitching the deer tail as I made my shot. No sooner had I hung the tail from a branch and settled into my ground blind than I saw the buck walking parallel to my back trail.

But for some reason he decided to take his usual route to the ravine and ledge. Before reaching the area where he typically started to travel down the ledge, he made a sharp turn and started down the ravine. I moved up to the edge and peaked down. The answer to why the buck had moved off so suddenly was a hot doe fifty yards below. He chased after her and they went up the other side. I watched as another buck with a slightly smaller rack chased my buck down the other side of the ridge and ran off with the doe.

The hunt was on again. I followed his track for exactly three hours back and forth over several ridges. Luckily, I leased the five hundred acres I was hunting, and it bordered another one hundred acres on which no one had permission to hunt. His tracks eventually led me back to the spot where I had previously jumped him.

Just as I crested the top of the ridge, I noticed that his tracks stopped on the side of the ridge. The tracks appeared to indicate that he had paced around and then headed toward the flat on top of the ridge. I circled off to the side and approached the knoll slowly, carefully scanning back and forth for him. Then I saw him looking over the ridge away from my direction and down into the ravine, almost like he expected me to be coming up any minute. The .50-caliber blast echoed across the mountain as the 200-grain sabot hit its mark. The big buck never lifted his head. He died in his bed, looking over the ledge for his pursuer. If I hadn't noticed how his tracks paused and then headed away, I would never have known to slow up and cut off to the side.

It's also worth noting that I knew when to quit the track that first day as darkness settled in. On the second day, I knew I didn't have the strength or the focus to stay on the track. And I knew I had him when I was able to read what his tracks meant the third day of this amazing hunt.

The buck had twelve points, and his antlers were heavy and palmated. His body was bone-thin, though, and when I tried to drag him out one of his antlers pulled off. I guessed that he was an old buck that had seen better days. I confirmed this when I sent a tooth to a lab and they aged it at an incredible ten years and six months old. No wonder he was hanging out in an area where

This buck was aged at an amazing ten years old. I wish I could've seen his rack in its prime at 6½ to 7½ years old.

younger bucks frequented. He was probably run out of his old haunts by other mature bucks that were now too strong for him.

In any case, being able to read sign from his track enabled me to take this handsome and savvy buck.

Chapter

3

TRACKING TIPS

The last few chapters have dealt primarily with the fundamentals of tracking deer, but now it's time to look at specific ways to use tracking to locate bucks for shot opportunities. This is the real "meat" of tracking, strategies that will put a buck in your crosshairs.

I'm sure many of you have heard and read that some hunters can always tell the difference between the tracks of a buck and a doe. Others, especially biologists, steadfastly believe that it is impossible to tell the difference between male and female tracks with absolute certainty. I agree with this, but only in a general sense.

BUCK VERSUS DOE

There are indicators to help you differentiate a buck's track from a doe's: size, width, splay, and depth of the print. But hunters often overlook other factors that provide valuable clues. If you elevate your detective work to visualize not only the track itself but also the sign that surrounds it, you will, more often than not, be able to tell a buck track from a doe track. Let's start with the basics.

The extra wide spread of the two toes and the depth of the dewclaws of this track indicate that the deer is heavy and has a deep, stocky chest—two good signs that the track could belong to a mature buck. (Ted Rose)

TRACK SIZE

The first thing a tracker should look at is the size of the hoof print. No matter how big a doe is, she rarely achieves the body weight of a sizeable buck. Therefore, her track will only rarely be as large as a big buck's track. But an old doe that has made it through eight or more seasons may actually be big enough to leave a track that is very comparable to that of a mature medium-sized whitetail buck. In that case, you'll need to look for other indicators to confirm that you're onto a buck.

DEWCLAWS

If there are less than two or three inches of snow on the ground, a doe walking at a normal pace usually doesn't leave tracks with dewclaw marks. Not so with a mature buck. He always leaves tracks with dewclaw imprints, no matter how deep the snow. The heavier the buck is, the deeper the dewclaw's imprints will be in the snow. Keep in mind that if a deer has been running in the snow the dewclaw imprints will always be present, whether left by a buck or doe. Again, a good tracking detective will soon discover that a buck's dewclaws are larger in size than a doe's, even when running. And the dewclaws leave marks in the snow that exceed the width of the buck print itself.

These prints clearly show that the buck was walking and unworried about his back trail. So I kept a slow pace and concentrated on scanning the terrain ahead.

DISTANCE BETWEEN PRINTS

Another good indicator of whether or not you're following a mature buck is the distance between the left and right prints. If the spread is eight inches, you're on a good-sized buck. Ten inches, and you're really onto something. And at twelve inches or more, you're on the trail of a trophy-class whitetail.

This is a mature, healthy, well-conditioned whitetail. There is no doubt that his track would be deep, wide, long, and splayed. (Ted Rose)

As a buck matures, several physical characteristics can help you estimate his age. At 3½ years old, a buck's chest appears deeper than its hindquarters, giving it the appearance of a well-conditioned racehorse. At 4½ years old, his fully muscled neck blends into the shoulders, and his waistline is as deep as his chest. At 5½ to 6½ years, a buck's neck blends completely into its shoulders and the front of its body appears to be one large mass. Once a buck passes 6½ years, its tracks are often mistaken for a younger buck's due to the decreasing amount of muscularity in its shoulders.

So the distance between tracks changes as the buck matures. The deeper chest eventually puts more weight on his forelegs and often causes him to have a long, flat-footed stride.

WALKING STYLE

If a buck is dragging his hooves while walking, even in a very light snowfall, it's a good bet that he's an older buck. Older deer—4½ years and up—have a tendency to drag their feet more than younger bucks.

In deeper snow, all deer appear to drag their feet. Bucks still drag their feet more than does, but it's difficult to make the distinction once several inches of snow are on the ground.

I've noticed something similar when hunting on dry, dusty *sundaroes* in Texas. There is always a top layer of loose soil where a buck's prints are sharp and identifiable, yet older bucks still tend to drag their hooves, even in this type of terrain.

A buck usually swaggers when he walks. The greater the swagger, the bigger the buck. Unlike a doe, which will travel under and through brush, a big buck is more likely to go around such vegetation to avoid entangling his antlers. This is especially true for wide-racked bucks. Still, some bucks are just too lazy to go around an obstacle and instead push their way through it. In this instance, it's important to notice how a buck moves through the brush. Usually, one hoof will be off to the side as he maneuvers to work his rack through the vegetation. A good tracking detective deciphers small clues like this to help interpret the track he's following.

URINE

A buck urinates as he walks, leaving dribble marks in the snow. I often laugh to myself when I see this because it reminds me of men over fifty years old who have prostate problems. Dribbling becomes part of everyday life for older males, bucks and men alike.

A buck urinates like this because he's leaving scent marks as he travels through areas. We've all seen a dog marking each and every tree or hydrant on his morning walk. A buck basically does the same thing.

These dribbled urine marks can sometimes stretch three to five feet. A doe, on the other hand, will almost always squat and urinate in one place. Even when a buck is urinating just to relieve himself, the urine leaves a different pattern. Doe urine will be concentrated in a relatively small spot, and the urine mark will show up behind, or centered on, her tracks. A buck's urine appears in front of his tracks. As any male knows, the penis is not as stationary as we would sometimes like it to be. The buck's hanging appendage wobbles around like an out-of-control fire hose, causing urine to scatter over a large area. Although this makes it sound as if the urine spreads over quite a distance, I'm really only talking about several inches.

Use your nose when following a large track, especially during the rut. A big, mature whitetail's urine exudes a strong, musky odor. It will be unmistakable once you've learned to recognize it. While hunting with friends over the years, I've often stopped in my tracks and taken a long, deep sniff of the air. In almost every case I've been able to find a urine mark in the snow or, even on bare ground, in a scrape. The odor of fresh urine is so powerful that it can be tasted in the molecules of the air. This may seem hard to believe, but I promise you that once you've learned to identify this scent, you will notice it on future hunts.

Picking up this scent is a matter of experience, and it pays big dividends for hunters who pay attention. It can direct you to a hot primary scrape, the trail of a buck following a doe, a buck's core area, and many times right to his midday bed.

OTHER TYPES OF SIGN

Some sign is more subtle than just plain tracks. These clues are harder to see, especially for the novice tracker, so they often go unnoticed. This is unfortunate, because such sign can provide valuable information about things like the direction the buck is heading, how big his antlers are, if he's after a doe, and much more.

To discover this information, a tracker needs to do more than follow a buck's hoof prints. A lot of hunters become so mesmerized by the hoof prints that they often overlook other equally important messages the deer leaves behind.

ANTLER MARKS IN SNOW

I once tracked a set of hoof prints that were wide and set deep in the snow, with splayed toes. This indicated to me that the track probably belonged to a mature buck. Back then, as long as a buck had points on his rack he was fair game as far as I was concerned. So I set out after the prints in earnest. After a few hours of walking all over the mountain, I was ready to give up. The weather was getting colder and I only had a couple hours of light left. Just then, I happened to look more closely at the track in front of me, which was at the base of a log where the buck had been nibbling on some fungus.

I clearly saw his nose print in the snow. As I examined it carefully, I noticed that the tips of his antlers were imprinted in the snow on either side of the nose print. This really caught my attention because the tips from the main beams typically don't leave marks in the snow. It's usually the second, third, and fourth tines (if any) that leave their mark.

I pulled out my tiny tape measure, which is always in my pack, and discovered that the points were twenty-two inches from tip to tip. I also saw several other marks in the snow that were obviously from other tines on his rack. To quit following his trail now was absolutely out of the question.

I jumped the buck just an hour later. Unfortunately, this was one of those occasions where the chase ended with the buck escaping. My mind had been briefly diverted by studying his track *too* hard, and the buck jumped up from behind a blowdown and ran off before I could get a shot off.

I didn't come home with a deer that day, but I did learn something about judging a buck's antlers by the impressions left in the snow. As mentioned above, the marks are usually left by the second, third, and fourth tines—not the brow tines or the tips of the main beams. So if you see an impression with three points on each side, the buck you're trailing is most likely a ten-pointer.

As an interesting aside, bucks lying in their beds typically leave an imprint of just one side of their antlers in the snow. Seasoned hunters, and some biologists, believe that this usually occurs on the left side of the buck's head, as most bucks lie to the left when sleeping. Knowing this doesn't necessarily help the tracker, but it certainly doesn't hurt.

BACK PRINTS IN THE FRONT

Neophyte trackers are often confused about whether they're looking at the front or back hoof. But the truth is that you're always

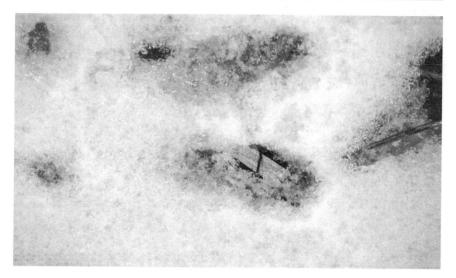

The back hoof of a deer is always smaller than the front hoof. (Ted Rose)

looking at the back hoof. The reason is simple. A deer—buck or doe—always puts its back foot in the same spot its front hoof just made. So the front track is always covered by the back one. And it pays to remember that the back hoof of a deer is always smaller than the front.

This helps you in two ways. First, you will quickly learn to look for unique markings on an individual deer's hoof print, such as chips, splits, shape, size, etc. Second, if you aren't sure about the track you're following, you'll know to stay with it until you come to a spot where the buck stops or mills about. When this happens, the buck will leave a front hoof print that you can size up to help determine how big he might be.

Once you've determined that the track you're on belongs to a buck of some size, you can once again take up the trail.

IS THE TRACK FRESH?

Every hunter wants to know how best to determine the freshness of tracks. But the only way to know with any certainty if tracks were left "only moments ago" is to actually see the buck standing in those tracks.

There are a lot of variables in aging a track in the snow or on bare ground. Wet snow helps keep the track sharp for a longer period than dry snow. Sometimes this can be problematic, because the tracker is led to believe the track is fresher than it actually is.

Ice build-up and wind have made these tracks hard to age accurately.

In a dry snow, you will often notice crystals of ice forming in the track. If you know how long the snow has been on the ground you'll be able to age the track more reliably.

Tracks blown over with new snow are the most difficult to age. Even the best of trackers will have a hard time locating and aging a good set of tracks in windy conditions.

You also must learn to identify tracks in snow that have been affected by warmer temperatures, or even rain. Under these conditions the tracks will look older, and in some instances melting snow will make them appear larger than they really are.

TRACKS AND SCAT

Here's where you separate the men from the boys, because this tactic requires the hunter to feel and smell deer droppings. Sometimes I squeeze the droppings between my fingers and break them apart to look for the type of forage the deer has been eating. Doing this may also give you a good idea of how close you are to the buck. On a cold day, droppings freeze more quickly than normal. The squishier and wetter the scat is, the fresher it is. When it has a mucous-like texture on the outside and a fresh odor, drop the crap and scan for the buck with your eyes. He may be very close.

I know many trackers who swear they can tell the difference between buck droppings and doe droppings by the size or consistency. Other seasoned trackers are adamant that there is no difference between scat that sticks together in clumps and individual pellets. I fall squarely in the middle of these two camps. As with everything else in tracking, clumpy scat and single pellet droppings are just small pieces of a larger puzzle. *Nothing* about tracking sign is absolute.

The consistency of droppings may vary from season to season as a result of what the animals are feeding on at a given time.

Although this deer scat appears large and clumped together, there isn't enough information to clearly identify whether it was left by a buck or doe. (Ted Rose)

In the summer, when foliage is greener, the droppings are more likely to be clumped together, which in and of itself tells you little about whether they come from a doe or buck. But I have noticed that a buck's scat is like everything else about a buck—whether it's his track, his chest, his stride, his neck—it is usually larger than a doe's. In the case of his poop, I'd like to delicately suggest that here, too, he has a heavier load.

Of course, this doesn't necessarily mean that he will leave a large, elongated clump of dung. I learned this when I started keeping my Deer Diary Stat cards in 1975. Each time I field dressed a decent-sized buck, I noticed the scat in his colon was usually composed of individual pellets.

I got so curious about this that I decided to do some research. Over the remainder of the year, I field dressed several fresh road-killed bucks to see if the colon material was consistent with what I found during the hunting season. It was. Each buck had single pellets in its colon. As the years passed, the stat cards

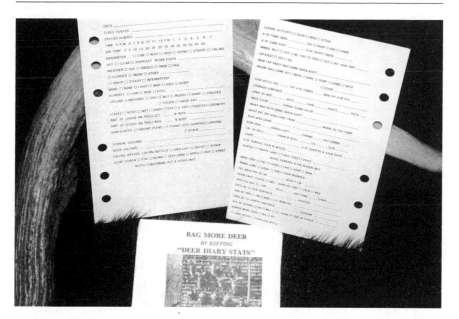

I use Deer Diary cards to record more than eighty different statistics and notes for each deer I bag. Over the years, they've become an invaluable part of my hunting success. (Call 1-800-652-7527 to order a set.)

clearly indicated that most of the time most of the bucks had single pellets in their colons. There were times when this didn't hold true, but not often enough to change the overall findings.

My records also confirmed that buck scat was larger than the pellets from does in the areas I hunt. This may be different in remote wilderness areas, but I wouldn't know because I do most of my tracking in farmlands or near the suburbs.

THE TRACKING EXPERIENCE

It bears repeating that most hunters, me included, tracking in real-world conditions are following bucks that will more than likely run into other hunters or enter private land at some point.

I mention this because the factors that go into the decision about whether or not to take up a trail are different for me than

These hunters shot their deer in the big woods of Maine, where they didn't have to worry much about inadvertently running the bucks into other hunters. (Hal Blood)

they are for trackers who live in places like Maine and Vermont. Time is against me and with them. The longer I'm on a trail, the less likely the tracking will end in the taking of the buck. That may be depressing to hear, but if you're tracking on a limited number of acres it's just reality. And if you want to be effective you must understand this early on. It will make you a better tracker in pressured hunting country and a very good tracker in wilderness areas.

Let me give you a comparison using big woods trackers (BWTs) and pressured woods trackers (PWTs). When a BWT takes up after a buck he has time to follow the quarry without a lot of pressure. PWTs don't have that benefit. The BWT can dog his prey for many hours without much care that he will run it into another hunter. Not so in the areas where a PWT hunts. Wilderness hunters can even react to sign differently than their PWT comrades.

Let's say either a BWT or PWT picks up a buck track early in the morning. They both can assume the buck is most likely bedded down. The BWT can now make a plan and head off on the trail. The PWT has to first take into account whether or not the buck is bedded down on land he can track on or if it's bedded on his neighbor's posted property.

If the BWT gets close to his buck and notices that the animal is picking up his tempo the BWT can, without much thought, pick up his pace as well. A PWT can't do that. He has to stop and think about where the buck is heading. If it is circling, he has a chance to continue following it despite the quick pace. If, on the other hand, the PWT determines that the buck is making a beeline toward another property he has to slow the chase and give the buck time to settle down. His only hope is that the buck circles back or remains within his hunting area; otherwise, the hunt has ended.

These are just a few of the many tactical tracking differences between the big woods tracker and the tracker who follows hoof prints within smaller plots of land. So don't become depressed when you lose a buck that moves out of your hunting area.

Hunters who trail deer in non-wilderness areas must understand that the buck they're tracking will eventually head onto posted land if pushed too hard or fast.

I also don't want you to feel like you're less than a good tracker if you don't score on the first several trails you take up. Wilderness trackers have a way of making a lot of other would-be, real-world trackers feel incompetent. I'm sure they don't mean to, but they do. No matter how skilled you are, you can't expect to shoot anything close to a majority of the bucks you track in heavily hunted areas of limited size.

In big woods country you should be able to increase your success rate to one in ten tracks you take up.

Killing a buck you've tracked is the ultimate deer hunting experience, one that requires a great deal of skill and invokes all our atavistic feelings. As trackers, we become one with our surroundings and with our quarry. We are the hunter and deer are the prey. We have stalked them fair and square on their home turf and under their rules, and we have come away better for it. Tracking teaches us to be patient, observant, diligent, and unrelenting hunters. Like our cavemen ancestors, we become the efficient predators all hunters strive to be.

Ted Rose

Chapter

4

WOUNDED DEER

Every dedicated, ethical deer hunter must be able to track a wounded animal by the blood trail or by other sign. As I pointed out in the opening chapter, even the most accurate shooters will face this situation at some point in their hunting careers, so it pays to gain as much knowledge and experience as possible in preparation.

Anytime you're hunting with a friend that wounds a deer, volunteer to help him trail it. Keep a low profile, especially if the hunter you're assisting is experienced in trailing wounded deer, but stay alert to what is happening. It is very important not to feel embarrassed about asking an experienced tracker questions regarding the sign left behind. Take the time to join in on tracking even when it means giving up some of your own valuable hunting time. The experience you gain will make you a more proficient hunter, a hunter others will respect and admire.

UNDERSTANDING ANATOMY

To become a good tracker of wounded deer you must first become intimately familiar with a deer's anatomy. This includes knowing everything you can about its internal organs and its

Kate tracked and shot this doe on our farm. She had to follow the blood trail to find and finish it off.

skeletal, muscular, arterial, and cardiovascular systems. It is also crucial to learn all you can about the deer's hide. Understanding where certain hair has come from on the animal will help you identify the part of the body you hit and help you make educated guesses about what the deer will do next, where it might go, and how long it might take to bed down or expire.

The skeletal structure of a whitetail is particularly important for the bowhunter, who might put a broadhead through bone.

There are times when a broadhead or other projectile fails to penetrate the body cavity, and the resulting wound is only superficial. If the proper techniques are employed from the onset, the good tracker has a chance of recovering the deer with a skeletal or muscular wound. And if you identify that the buck you shot has a superficial wound, your first obligation is to follow the deer to the best of your ability. Stay on the blood trail until you're close enough for a killing shot or until the trail absolutely evaporates and all other sign disappears.

Recovering a deer that has been hit in a non-vital area requires an in-depth understanding of the wound itself. Wounds from different parts of a deer's body typically leave different types of blood sign. The color of the blood can range from very dark—almost black—to light pink. Understanding the colors will help you quickly determine how to track your buck.

For instance, bright crimson blood calls for immediate tracking, while pinkish blood, especially with tiny bubbles in it, indicates that the deer was hit in the lungs and should be allowed to rest before pursuit.

KNOW YOUR DEER HAIR

Once a deer is hit, a good tracker marks the exact spot—or as close as possible—and immediately seeks to locate any hair that has fallen from the impact of the broadhead or bullet. This is where a lot of novice blood-trail trackers make their first mistake. They often look for blood before looking for hair. Always look for hair first.

I once wounded a deer high in the back. I knew this was where I'd hit the deer because of two clues I picked up at the site of the shot. There was an absence of blood, and there was a lot of hair on the ground. Looking closely at the hair, I noticed it was very coarse, long, and dark gray with black tips. I suspected

Carefully examining hair left at the hit site will help you determine exactly where the animal was hit. This information allows you to make a better decision about how long to wait before picking up the trail.

it was hair from the top of the deer's back, so I checked it against the pocket-sized deer hair identification chart I always carry. (This is a wallet-sized portfolio with deer hair laminated on white business-sized cards with descriptions for each type of hair and what part of the body it came from.) I quickly confirmed that the hair I found was from the top of the deer's back.

Often, deer hit high in the back won't begin to bleed until they run twenty-five to fifty yards. Knowing this, I began to slowly and carefully search for more sign as I picked up the track of the running deer on hard ground. It was easy to see the direction the deer had taken from the scattered leaves and kicked-up dirt left behind. Within a hundred yards, I found blood and was able to follow it until I found the wounded buck bedded down. I shot him just as he stood up.

Upon closer examination, I found I had hit him above the spine. While the wound had slowed him down, it wasn't a killing

The hair from this buck indicated I'd made a high back shot, so I gave him time to settle down before following up. I found him in his bed and took the final shot just as he got up.

shot. The buck would have eventually recovered. By being able to identify the hair and knowing that the blood trail was not far ahead of me, I was able to get a second chance at this buck. (See chapter 5 for more detailed information on assessing blood and hair sign.)

GO SLOW, BE VIGILANT

When it comes to following a wounded deer, I can absolutely guarantee you that all good things come to trackers who are extremely patient and diligent. You must move slowly and observe all sign. This includes not allowing too many of your hunting buddies to join in tracking the animal before you have established some crucial evidence: (1) where the buck was hit, indicated by the hair you find; and (2) the color of the blood and the direction in which the deer moved off, whether in snow or on bare ground. Letting others help you too early on, no matter how good their intentions, may cause all-important sign to be unintentionally disturbed or eliminated completely.

Some of the best advice I can give you is simply to focus on the job at hand. Stop for a moment. Take a deep breath, and release some of the excitement from the shot. Begin your assessment at the precise location where the deer was shot. Once you've located hair and blood on the ground, it's important to remember to keep looking for blood in other places. Check for sign on branches, brush, and hanging vegetation.

Your next task is to determine whether the track you're following is from a walking or running deer. And never assume anything about a wounded animal.

LOTS OF BLOOD DOESN'T MEAN DEAD

One of the biggest misconceptions about following a blood trail is that the heavier the blood trail, the greater the possibility that the deer was fatally hit. Through experience, hunters learn that this is not always the case. A deer often leaves a lot of blood sign when the wound is superficial.

Years ago, I shot a buck at a difficult angle from a tree stand. My bullet hit the deer and I saw it go down. I watched for several minutes as it lay motionless, and finally decided it was mortally wounded. As soon as I lowered my rifle the buck jumped to its feet and ran off. Approaching the site of the hit, I took my time looking for hair and blood. I found plenty of hair and an immediate blood trail. The deer hair was stiff, very coarse, dark gray with dark tips, and about 2½ inches long. This indicated that the buck had been shot in the brisket. I knew then and there that I would have a long tracking job. I'd have to pay strict attention to the trail ahead if I were to get a second shot at this buck.

My cousin, Ralph, joined me on the trail and we tracked the buck for several hundred yards. Eventually, his wound appeared to have plugged itself. This left us with only his tracks to follow on bare ground and through a few patches of snow left here and there. Occasionally, we found a droplet or two of blood where he had stood still to watch his back trail. The buck actually passed within twenty yards of fourteen of our tree stands along his escape route—and that's no exaggeration. Take a moment to think about that. It's a classic example of Murphy's Law. Somehow deer instinctively know where to go and where not to go in their attempt to escape.

The only stand he avoided, of course, was the one in which my wife was sitting. Eventually, the buck's trail took him onto private land. Unfortunately, we didn't have permission to hunt this property. As we stood there discussing who would go back to ask for permission from the landowner, we heard a single shot ring out from the woods less than a hundred yards ahead of us. As it turned out, the owner of the neighboring property shot the buck.

Understanding the blood, hair, and track sign that we were looking at enabled us to pursue the buck for a few hours. If he hadn't entered private property, we would have eventually gotten a second opportunity to finish him off.

Get to know the landowners around the property you hunt. Offer to help them put up their posted signs. Even if you don't hunt their land they may give you permission to trail a wounded deer onto their property if necessary.

BEHAVIOR

Some of the most frequent questions hunters ask about trailing a deer include when and where it will bed down, whether it'll travel uphill or down, and whether or not it'll go to water. Well, there are no absolutes when it comes to the behavior of a wounded deer, especially a mature buck. As any seasoned hunter knows, big bucks have a special tenacity for life. Because of this, they tend to die hard.

I have found that the body weight of the wounded animal often determines how far it moves before bedding down, or even how long it goes before succumbing to its wound.

I once shot a buck in my hometown in a spot I named "The Bowl." It's a unique area that often attracts mature bucks because of its extreme cover. This particular buck was about fifty yards from me and walking slowly. I stopped him with a blat call and took my shot. I could clearly see that I hit the buck in the boiler room (the lungs) and was absolutely sure I would recover him within a short distance. When I checked the location of impact, I found blood and hair that supported the idea that I had made an excellent shot. Again, I was confident I would find the buck very quickly. But I did not.

I followed a heavy blood trail until the end of the day, when it got too dark to trail him any farther. I did everything right. I gave the buck enough time to bed down. And I moved slowly and methodically, keeping my eyes on the cover in front of me. But each time I got close to the buck, I saw or heard him slip away. I decided to let the buck bed down overnight, hoping I'd find him the next morning.

I picked up his blood trail at first light. To my utter amazement, I found the buck bedded but still alive. He strained to get up, but he was, for all intents and purposes, dead on his feet. One final shot dropped him in his tracks.

After field dressing the deer, I was stunned to see that I had indeed hit him squarely in the boiler room. The bullet entered through the rib cage, took out a lung, and ricocheted into the liver. I have no idea how the buck survived as long as he did.

I have experienced similar situations with other mature bucks over the years. The old adage "big bucks die hard" should

I shot this big buck in the lungs with a 180-grain bullet from a .30-06, but he still managed to travel several hundred yards before lying down and dying in his bed.

be remembered by anyone trailing a mature wounded whitetail buck. Whether it is hit with a broadhead or bullet, a deer's tenacity for life enables it to perform feats that younger deer simply can't.

Never become disillusioned when you hit a big buck well, only to find a long and arduous tracking job ahead. The simple fact is that big deer have more stamina than their smaller brethren and use that energy in amazing ways.

BEDDING DOWN

Deer that are severely hit look to bed down in thick cover as soon as they can. Even when shot in open hardwoods, a deer often moves to the security of a dense area before deciding to bed down. This behavior sometimes changes, though, if a deer detects a tracker following it.

Experience has taught me that wounded bucks tend to seek out certain types of dense cover. Ralph and Leo Somma, my long-time hunting companions, have substantiated this. Both of these hunters have tracked their fair share of wounded deer. Ralph lives and hunts in an area of New Jersey that's loaded with horse and agricultural farms surrounded by dense cover. Leo lives and hunts on the eastern part of Long Island, also in areas filled with dense cover. We also have a wide variety of terrain on our farms in upstate New York.

The bucks we've tracked, whether in New Jersey, Long Island, southern New York, or even central New York, have all headed to thick cover soon after being hit. Believe it or not, dense cover includes standing fields of corn. To a wary old buck, standing corn represents security. He instinctively knows that he can hide there safely. Be cautious when tracking a wounded deer into such areas. It's hard to locate blood in a cornfield when the ground is bare. Be observant, and look for blood smeared on the stalks and leaves of the corn.

No matter what the terrain, wounded deer will head to the thickest cover around. A deer hopes that the pursuers either pass it by or find it too hard to penetrate the cover. I have often seen hard-hit bucks use thick, nasty cover to bed in when they know they're being followed. As soon as they enter cover like this, they bed down. Often, a buck will rise from its bed, go thirty yards or so, and then bed down again because of its wound. So whenever

This buck is bedded at the edge of a swamp in the type of cover deer often seek out when wounded. Note that he's watching his back trail.

you find a bed with blood in it, be vigilant. I always recommend standing in the spot and slowly eyeballing the area carefully before picking up the trail again. Paying attention to this detail may put the wounded buck back in your sights.

UPHILL AND DOWN

There seems to be a never-ending controversy about whether deer travel uphill or downhill after being wounded. There is no perfect answer, and I can only relate to you what I've witnessed while tracking deer.

I've trailed many wounded bucks up the side of a mountain, despite the fact that most experts will tell you that a wounded deer rarely, if ever, heads uphill. One thing I discovered about tracking wounded deer uphill is that the blood trail is typically smaller than the blood trail left on level ground or when heading downhill. Why? I don't know. But it is a fact.

One opening morning my wife shot a buck at the base of a mountain behind our old house. She called on the radio to let me know that the buck had run off into the pines. She was going to wait fifteen minutes and then pick up the blood trail. About a half hour later, she called me back to let me know she was about two hundred yards into the blood trail and that the deer was heading halfway up the side of the ridge. Kate mentioned that she was worried the buck wasn't mortally wounded because the blood sign was dwindling. Knowing about the phenomenon of the diminishing uphill blood trail, I asked her to stop and wait for me.

We took up the blood trail and followed it another two hundred yards up the ridge to the first plateau. I asked Kate to stay behind while I carefully peeked over the top to look around the plateau for more blood sign. Within seventy-five yards I had picked up a lot of blood. Kate rejoined me and again we took up the trail. The blood remained significant for another hundred yards or so, until the buck started up toward the next plateau.

He must have been running out of gas because we found him bedded just thirty yards from where he walked onto the plateau, lying with his head flat on the ground.

Kate didn't even have to take a finishing shot. The buck expired in his bed within a few minutes. Upon field dressing him, we found out that her shot was indeed a fatal wound that should have left a significant amount of blood throughout the entire trail. Yet we only found an easy-to-follow blood trail on flat ground.

The blood trail of a wounded deer heading downhill always seems to be the same as one on flat terrain. I've never been able to put my finger on exactly why this is. You would think that because the deer is exerting itself more while walking uphill its heart would beat faster and therefore pump out more blood. But that's just not the case.

Another example of a wounded deer's ability to turn conventional wisdom on its head was documented on a TV show I produced in Canada back in 1988. Thousands of viewers saw a large-bodied, 140- to 155-class buck race uphill after being shot.

I hit the buck in the chest, and he immediately took off in high gear through a woodlot. The camera followed the action as the buck ran through the woods for about a hundred yards, down an embankment, through a small stream, and then up a very steep embankment on the other side toward an open field. As the buck started up the steep hill, it was obvious that his back legs were giving way. Yet he continued his ascent with a mindset that seemed irreversible.

Just shy of the top of the hill, about fifty yards above the stream, the buck's life force began to ebb. He collapsed. To our surprise, he staggered back to his feet and turned to look down toward the stream. At that point, I figured he was going to head downhill to the water. Instead, he tried to climb the last several yards uphill.

Within a dozen yards, the buck's back legs slowly gave out and he slid all the way back down the hill and into the stream. I believe he died on his feet as he tried to climb the last few yards of the steep embankment. Why the buck chose to run up this steep hill rather than staying on level ground or running along the stream is beyond me. But it proved once again that every deer's reaction to being wounded is unique.

SEEKING WATER

When it comes to a wounded deer heading for water, I can only repeat what I've touched on above: anything is possible. Most fatally hit deer, especially mature bucks, don't immediately head toward water. They simply aren't thinking about liquid at this

Wounded deer are unafraid of water, occasionally crossing swift currents or great depths while trying to escape. They often don't seek out water to drink, though, until the wound makes them feverish. (Ted Rose)

point. Instead, they are preoccupied with escape and survival. Not until a deer becomes feverish does it typically seek water. This typically occurs when a deer has a fatal wound that allows it to survive several hours or more, or when the wound is minor. In either case, the wound is serious enough to raise the deer's temperature.

Ted Rose

Chapter

5

BODY LANGUAGE

Hunters who've wounded deer often remark that they don't know where they hit the deer—which is quite understandable. In the heat of the moment, not everyone is able to actually follow the arrow or bullet to where it strikes the animal. There is a way, however, to quickly zero in on where your projectile hit the deer even before you begin to search for sign: watch how the buck or doe reacts after it is hit.

Deer almost universally react the same way to being hit in certain areas. Observe whether the buck jumps wildly into the air, hunches its back, lunges forward, or displays other distinct body language. By watching the body language, you can also determine if the hit was lethal. It may even help you find your deer faster.

In the last chapter I described the basic elements of following up wounded deer. Now it's time to take a closer look at how the blood trail and hair left at the hit site can be combined with observations of body language to pinpoint the type of wound and how this will affect the tracking job ahead.

THE LUNG SHOT

When a deer is shot through both lungs, it usually lunges forward and then takes off in a hard run. Its tail is held up about halfway for the first fifty yards or so, and the blood sign is usually found within fifty to seventy-five yards, if not right at the hit site. The color of the blood makes it easy to identify a lung shot, because it is often pink and has bubbles in it. I have also noticed that a deer hit in both lungs holds its belly low to the ground.

Deer hit in only one lung are often a tracking nightmare. I've seen several single-lunged bucks escape even the best trackers. These deer are eventually taken down by predators or other hunters because they are unable to move normally.

My cousin, Ralph, once shot a buck whose blood trail led us to wrongly believe we would recover it over the next rise or in the next blowdown. Unfortunately, that is a very common scenario when tracking deer hit in only one lung. The blood trail is profuse, but it seldom leads to recovery unless you're fortunate enough to jump the deer after it has bedded down and get a follow-up shot.

Ralph's buck was killed three days later by a neighboring apple farmer who was about to call it a day that morning when he noticed a buck slowly walking through the woods. He told us its gait was "labored and unusual." He could see that the buck had been previously wounded, and when he field dressed it he saw the wound channel through one lung.

As it turned out, the farmer also found Ralph's bullet and gave it to me. It had expanded more than it should have. This led me to believe that my cousin's bullet most likely hit an obstacle—such as a small branch—prior to entering the buck. Because the bullet had already expanded somewhat before impact, it only took out one lung. Otherwise, I believe its placement would have ensured a killing, double-lung shot.

THE HEART SHOT

If you shoot a deer near the brisket just behind the front leg, you've probably hit the heart. While the heart shot is a killing shot, I try to avoid it for a variety of reasons, especially when bowhunting. First, it's a small target in a difficult area that Mother Nature has protected well. If the shot is just a few inches low you could leave the deer with a non-fatal wound—and have a

This deer's body language told me exactly where I'd hit him. The recovery went smoothly as a result.

long tracking job ahead. Or you could miss the deer entirely. I prefer the larger target area presented by the lungs.

Also, the heart-shot deer I've taken over the years have traveled farther and faster than lung-shot deer. I've followed a few heart-shot deer that even traveled more than two hundred yards before dying. Some have taken a long time to expire, and have done so while bedded.

A fine shot from a bowhunter often only cuts into the heart or nicks the heart muscle. Deer with this type of wound can live for an hour or more.

Blood from heart-shot deer is often found within yards of where the animal was standing when hit. The distinctive crimson-red blood also helps confirm the location of the wound. When beginning to track a heart-shot deer, look for blood a few feet away from the trail because blood can spray from the animal's wound as it runs away. The deer typically bleeds continuously, causing a profuse blood trail.

The body language of a heart-shot deer is common to other big game animals shot in the heart. The deer jumps into the air and kicks its rear hooves back. Upon impact, the deer usually runs hard but in an erratic line.

THE NECK SHOT

For many years, I thought taking a neck shot with a firearm made a fast, fatal hit as long as a couple of elements fell into place. The deer had to be within fifty yards, and it had to be standing still. If this was the case, I was reasonably sure that my bullet would hit all the vitals necessary to make an instant kill. A shot that hits the carotid artery, jugular vein, and the vertebrae in the neck is devastating. In most instances, it also takes out the windpipe and neck muscles. The deer usually drops in its tracks when hit like this.

There is, however, a downside to shooting deer in the neck. If the shot misses the vitals and only hits muscle, the odds of recovering the deer are small. And if only the windpipe is hit—depending upon how badly it's damaged—the deer could escape.

There isn't much to say about the body language of a deer hard hit in the vitals of the neck. It's almost as if you took a sledgehammer to the back of its head. The deer usually drops in its tracks. In the event that it doesn't, you may see air bubbles in bright crimson blood. The trailing job rarely lasts more than fifty yards.

ABDOMINAL WOUNDS

Abdominal wounds are not the same as gut shots or paunch shots. Abdominal hits often involve organs like the liver and kidneys. Kidney-shot deer usually die within sixty seconds. Often there will be trauma to more than one organ, which means various shades of blood on the trail.

Deer shot in the liver die more slowly, but they do die. Sometimes it takes the animal several hours to succumb to the wound. These deer often leave very coarse, medium-length, dark-brown or gray hair with black tips at the hit site. I mention this because the best possibility of finding hair from a liver shot is at the impact site.

The blood of a liver-shot deer is dark red. You usually find it within fifty yards of the hit, although only rarely right at the hit site. The deer most often lunges ahead at the shot and then quickly runs away. Unlike deer hit in the stomach or intestines, which usually run away slowly, liver-hit deer beat it out of there.

STOMACH WOUNDS

A stomach wound often misleads the hunter into thinking the deer is not fatally hit. A majority of the time, stomach wounds are fatal.

The hair left from a stomach hit will be very coarse, of medium length, and brown or gray with lighter tips. Hair from the bottom of the deer is white or light gray, coarse, slightly twisted, and long.

The blood trail from a stomach wound is dark red—lighter than the blood from an intestinal hit but darker than the blood from a liver-shot deer—and the contents of the sign are solid and usually tan in color. If the deer is hit in the intestines, however, the sign will be liquid, slick, and most often dark brown or green. A paunch-shot deer's blood may contain contents from the stomach or intestines.

When hit in the stomach, a deer exhibits distinct body language. It jumps, hunches up its back, walks off a few steps, and then remains standing for a few moments, often wobbling, before walking off. Another good indicator is that its legs are usually spread wide as it walks off, and its neck is usually stretched out even with the line of its back.

Some stomach-hit deer can take up to twenty-four hours to die. These deer often head for heavy cover to bed down. Don't expect to find a lot of blood from stomach-hit deer.

INTESTINAL WOUNDS

Deer hit in the intestines will die, but it may take up to thirty-six hours or so. They often travel a long distance before bedding down, and the blood trail is difficult to follow. The hair from an intestinal wound is the same as the hair left from a stomach wound. The sign left contains the darkest of blood, sometimes appearing black or very dark maroon. Sign at the site of the hit usually doesn't contain blood. Most often, the blood trail begins fifty to seventy-five yards away. A deer hit in the intestines reacts with body language almost identical to that of stomach-hit deer.

ARTERIAL WOUNDS

At seminars, I always get a lot of questions about wounds to the primary arteries, including the carotid, the aorta, and the femoral. Let me say right up front that wounds to any of these arteries with either a broadhead or bullet will cause profound bleeding and an amazingly quick death to the deer. But that doesn't necessarily translate into a simple blood trail in every case. Depending on the deer's reaction and the specific artery hit, the trail can run from just a few feet to one hundred yards or so.

It's important to note that I'm not talking about injuries to smaller arteries or veins here. I'm referring to the severing of major arteries. A deer must lose about 30 percent of its blood before bleeding to death. So you can see how drastic a wound must be for a deer to die within seconds of the artery being cut. While most wounds bring on shock, an arterial wound causes a deer to go into shock very fast because the blood leaves the deer's body so quickly.

All arterial wounds leave bright-red blood. The deer leaves a significant amount of blood on the ground and on vegetation, as the bleeding is profuse externally and internally. The harder the deer runs, the quicker the bleed-out occurs. While blood from the aortic artery leaves sign on both sides of the deer's trail— sometimes up to twelve to eighteen inches away—wounds from the carotid or femoral arteries cause blood to fall close to the tracks of the deer.

I have shot several bucks in the femoral artery with a broad-head, but I only take the shot when this small target is close enough to put the odds heavily in my favor. I never shoot for this artery unless the deer is ten yards or less from my stand. This is a devastating hit. I have watched deer shot in the femoral artery die in less than thirty seconds, some even faster.

I grunted this eight-pointer to within fifteen yards, where he offered me a perfect shot at the femoral artery (a target that's only appropriate in rare instances). The buck trotted ten yards, sat down, rolled over, and died in less than three minutes.

The last deer I shot in the femoral artery was taken on a 100-acre woodlot in Warwick, New York, during an unusually warm rut. It was a sunny morning with temperatures in the sixties, and I was fortunate enough to see a few racked bucks chasing a single doe. I had my natural deer tail decoy hanging below the stand, and I was using a soft estrus blat call to encourage one of the bucks to leave the doe and come to me.

It worked on the smallest of the three bucks. Breaking off from the other two, the buck trotted toward me. He stood facing away less than ten yards from my stand. He was staring at my flickering deer tail, so I drew back and released my arrow. It hit the buck on the inside of his hindquarters, right where I was aiming.

I immediately knew I'd hit the femoral artery, as blood began to flow profusely from the wound. The buck jumped and started to run away. To my amazement, after running ten yards he stopped, wobbled back and forth, and sat down on his haunches. Within seconds he collapsed onto his side and expired.

On another hunt, a trophy-class buck walking away from me offered no other shot than its rear side or inside its legs. The buck was about thirty yards from me and was standing still, about to enter some thick brush. My scope was already planted on his femoral artery and I fired. Normally, I would let a lesser buck go rather than ruin a lot of the meat with a shot like this. But this buck's rack was large enough that I was willing to settle for a substantial amount of meat rather than all of it.

Upon firing, I watched the deer jump high off the ground and kick out his rear leg. He landed in a stagger and then ran off. Within ten seconds I heard him crash to the forest floor. Twenty seconds after that, the buck stopped thrashing its legs and died.

Ethically, you must be careful about shooting a deer in this area. If you miss the femoral artery, you can cause a grave wound to the animal. When an arterial shot is not placed perfectly, the deer may escape and die of its wounds far from the site of the hit.

Any hunter who decides to take such a shot must show strong discipline. For bowhunters, this means passing on arterial target areas beyond a range of ten yards. And rifle hunters should never aim for these areas if the deer isn't standing still within thirty yards. Also, I can't stress enough that this is not a shot any beginner or novice hunter should take under any circumstances.

A deer has about one ounce of blood for each pound of total body weight. So an average 150-pound buck has about 150 ounces of blood in its body, or a little over nine pints. As a deer's heart can pump about 120 to 160 cc's of blood per beat, it can bleed out quickly if all the elements are in place. Half of the deer's blood is filled with oxygen from the lungs that is then delivered to the cells through the arteries. The other half carries carbon dioxide being returned through the veins. A human without oxygen can live about three to four minutes before losing consciousness. The same is true for deer.

Deer hit by broadheads tend to leave a better blood trail. They hemorrhage to death. Bullets often leave a more difficult blood trail to follow because the bullet's impact makes a greater wound in the surrounding muscle tissue and organs. The deer usually succumbs to the trauma and shock more quickly with a bullet hit, which makes the animal easier to locate.

WHITETAIL DEER HAIR IDENTIFICATION

Read your deer's body language after the shot, and then use the blood trail and hair left at the hit site to confirm the type of wound made. This information will make tracking the injured buck much easier. I always carry a pocket-sized hair identification chart to help with this task.

Heart Shot: The hair will be long and brown, with grayish guard hairs. Wait at least twenty minutes before trailing.

Spine Shot: Although this deer will drop in his tracks, a second "finishing" shot may be needed, so approach cautiously. The hair left behind will be long and light tan with black tips.

Loin Shot: A hit just above the kidney area and below the back of the spine will cause major damage to the aortic artery. There will be a major blood trail to follow, and the hair will be long and dark with black tips.

Lung Shot: The blood trail will be strong and will have bubbles in it. The hair will be coarse and brown.

Kidney Shot: This wound will bleed a lot right away. The hair will be long, dark brown, and may sometimes have black tips.

Liver Shot: The hair at the hit site will be coarse, short, and light tan or brown with reddish-brown tips.

Brisket Shot: This wound usually leaves a lot of blood at first, but plugs up within two hundred yards. The hair will be curly and grayish white. Deer hit here are seldom recovered, as this isn't a fatal injury.

Continued on next page

Gut Shot: The hair from this hit will be coarse, short, and light in color with reddish-brown tips.

Neck Shot: This hair will be short, coarse, and light tan, especially if it's from the lower neck area. It gradually becomes darker with black tips farther up the neck.

Belly Shot: Look for long white curly hairs that are hollow.

High Back Shot: The hair from this hit will be long, dark, and black-tipped.

Rear Shot: The hair found at the hit site will be short, white, fine, and have curly tips. This deer can be trailed immediately.

Calls and Calling

Ted Rose

Chapter

6

DEER CALLS

One of the chapters that received the most response in my first book *Whitetail Strategies* was "How to Use Deer Calls Effectively." Many of the folks who e-mailed me after reading the book remarked how their deer hunting had improved after they began using deer calls. Some ardent trackers even told me that by adding calling to their arsenal, they were able to see and bag more deer.

Deer calls have always been underrated and underused. I believe this can be attributed to the way many of us were taught to hunt deer by our fathers, uncles, and grandfathers. A lot of hunters from the older generation are ardent believers in not making any noise that might spook a deer in the woods, including sounds that deer naturally make. Trying to convince these old-timers that using deer calls can improve their hunting skills has been frustrating for me. No matter how many times they've been shown the effectiveness of deer calls through my television show, magazines articles, or in my books, these dyed-in-the-wool anti-callers remain steadfast in their belief that using calls to attract, hold, or intentionally roust deer is foolhardy at best and a bunch of malarkey at worst. But they couldn't be more mistaken.

Using deer calls has consistently improved my ability to see and take bucks. It is by far the most natural strategy a hunter can use, although it isn't a foolproof strategy that works every time out. Still, I've employed deer calls more than any other tactic during my many years of hunting across North America.

In order to be an effective deer caller, you must first learn how to mimic the primary vocalizations deer make. Practicing each cadence of each of the vocalizations long before opening day will give you the confidence necessary to place a call in your

The whitetail bucks in this part of my trophy room were all bagged using deer calls. Even the moose, caribou, and gobbler were called in. (So far, my young lab hasn't responded.)

mouth and blow without worrying about whether the noise will be beneficial or harmful to your chances. When you call correctly, you'll definitely attract more deer. Once you gain this mindset, you'll incorporate deer calls into your hunting strategy season after season with amazing success.

Back in the 1960s, using calls to attract deer was a well-kept secret known only to seasoned, savvy woodsmen who hunted remote wilderness areas of North America, especially in Quebec, Canada. These hunters used rudimentary calls made of rubber bands and balsa wood to regularly attract whitetails, but they rarely talked about them.

It was one of these cagey old hunters who first introduced me to deer calls early in my hunting life. I was sitting on a stand overlooking a swamp in New York's Adirondack Mountains. Every so often I heard a soft lamb-like bleat. I had no idea what the sound was or what was making it. But I did know that every fifteen minutes or so the sound emanated from a dip about one hundred yards below the ledge I was sitting on.

Since this was only my second year of deer hunting, my patience level wasn't very high. If I didn't see a deer within the first hour or two, I usually got up and skulked around hoping to jump a buck. I still smile when I think about my impatience in those days. It never seemed to fail; as soon as I got up and started walking around, I'd hear a shot ring out close by. I'm sure I unknowingly drove a lot of bucks to a lot of other hunters back then.

In any event, by 7:30 that morning my patience had waned and I was determined to find out what was making that noise. As I stood up, I heard the sound again. This time, however, I heard a similar noise coming from the swamp in the opposite direction. A big doe emerged from the swamp and trotted toward the ledge below me. Never swerving, she went straight to the source of the noise.

I watched as she stopped and then began pacing nervously back and forth. Then the excitement started. Two bucks ran out of the swamp, hot on her trail. I started shaking and was still trying to decide which one to shoot when a gunshot rang out. The bigger of the two bucks dropped in its tracks. I threw my .30-30 to my shoulder and attempted to draw a bead on the second buck as he and the doe weaved and darted through the hardwoods, but there was no chance to pull the trigger. Naturally, I was shocked at what had just taken place.

As I sat there disgusted, a hunter who had been posted well below me stood and approached the downed buck. I grabbed my gear and went down to talk to him. I soon discovered that this old gentleman had been the source of the doe blats I'd heard all morning.

This veteran hunter told me he regularly used a doe bleat to call in bucks like the eight-pointer shown here.

The Olt deer call was the first call I learned to use to talk to deer. It has worked successfully for many years.

He told me that he'd been using doe blats to attract whitetails for many years, especially "to pull bucks from heavy cover" like the swamp we were overlooking. He laughed until there were tears in his eyes when I told him I thought I was posted near a sheep farm. "Boy," he said, "there ain't a sheep or a farm between Childwold and Tupper Lake, and they're thirty miles apart!"

While he field dressed his eight-point buck, I stood there in amazement as he told me story after story of how successful he had been over the years using a blat call. "Hell, boy, if you wanna kill bucks like this, learn to blow one of these here doe calls," he said, placing an Olt deer call in my hand. "Your friends will think you're crazy for using it, but I betcha it'll work."

I bought an Olt call that afternoon in a tiny general store in Tupper Lake during a heavy snowfall. I blew it on almost every hunting trip that season without success. But I didn't give up. The memory of that morning's hunt and the old gent's stories remained vivid, so I continued to use and practice the doe blat call.

Within a few short years, I became proficient with a blat call and some of the other deer vocalizations. I had enough reaction from deer to know that I was onto a tactic that could provide me with more success than just sitting and waiting for a buck to pass my stand. I promised myself that through trial and error and continuous practice I would gain the experience and confidence needed to become an accomplished deer caller.

Over the next thirty-five years, I did just that. I learned all thirteen primary vocalizations that deer make and the myriad sub-calls, also known as cadences, that go along with each one. I practiced in spring and summer when deer are easy to see along roads and in fields. I made bleats, blats, snorts, and even grunts,

I've had good results with a variety of deer blat calls over the years. The Deer Stopper from E.L.K., Inc. is one of my favorites. (Kate Fiduccia)

This buck is vocalizing to the doe with soft, guttural grunts, a common sound throughout the deer woods during the breeding season. (Ted Rose)

and I watched their reactions to each call. I learned that there was a definite difference between a blat and a bleat. I saw deer react in many different ways to a variety of snorts. And I discovered that does even grunt during the off-season.

Learning how vocal deer really are gave me the confidence I needed to use calls during the archery and firearm seasons. After all, if deer "talked" to each other as much as I had witnessed during the spring and summer, why wouldn't they continue to communicate during the most important time for does and bucks — the rut.

It became apparent to me that any hunter who resists learning how to use vocalizations to attract deer is only hurting himself. He is missing out on what I've long referred to as one of Mother Nature's natural seductions. Whitetails aren't the only

These deer calls imitate common variations of the primary snort, blat, bleat, and grunt.

ruminants that respond to calls. All thirty species and subspecies of deer in the Americas vocalize and respond readily to the sounds made by hunters using deer calls.

CALLS YOU NEED TO KNOW

While biologists have recognized thirteen primary deer vocalizations, there are four basic sounds a hunter must incorporate into his bag of tricks in order to see and tag more deer. Thankfully, they are the easiest of all the vocalizations to learn and mimic. These sounds include the snort, the blat, the bleat, and the grunt.

Each one of these has a variety of sub-calls (cadences) that mean something other than the primary vocalization. For instance, the blat has five cadences: the alarm blat, the feeding blat, the locating blat, the trail blat, and the social blat. As you become more experienced, you can start learning and adding these sub-vocalizations to the four primary calls to make yourself a more complete deer caller.

I'll go over each primary call and its sub-calls in detail in the chapters ahead. I advise you to learn each thoroughly. Doing so will improve your deer hunting success immediately and exponentially. But first let's look at some general principles related to calling.

TALKING TO DEER IN SPRING

Each spring, I practice using bleat calls to attract does. It is important to understand the difference between bleats and blats. A bleat is made by fawns from birth to about eighteen months of age. At that point, the fawn's voice changes much like a teenager's. The bleat evolves into a deeper-toned call known as a blat. Be cautious about this, as there are times when an adult deer will respond negatively if you're trying to imitate a blat and it comes out sounding like a bleat.

The spring is a good time to practice because adult does are most vocal after giving birth to fawns. A fawn's neonatal vocalizations are crucial to its survival. The different cadences made by a fawn include a feeding bleat, an alarm bleat, and a locating bleat. There are also more subtle types of bleat calls made by fawns to demonstrate a wide variety of emotions such as pleasure, discontent, and so on. The doe readily reacts to any of the vocalizations a fawn makes. It is nature's way of making the doe a better caretaker of her offspring.

KEEP IT LOW

An experienced caller learns how to call softly. Occasionally, a louder sound may be necessary. On very rare occasions, a more aggressive call may be the key to success. But if there is one thing I can promise you about calling, it's that a hunter who makes loud, aggressive vocalizations to does and/or bucks, even mature bucks, will scare away more deer than he attracts. Many times, a hunter will never hear or see the deer approaching over the noise he's making, or worse yet, won't even get the deer interested enough to respond because his calling has frightened it away.

Deer react negatively to loud, aggressive vocalizations, even when they're as far away as two hundred yards. Loud calls are unnatural in the deer world, so they usually interpret them to mean trouble is afoot. When faced with an alien sound, deer will fade away into the cover like ghosts.

I often refer to the phrase "common sense hunting strategies" to help hunters relate to a specific tactic. I'm sure many hunters have been tempted by merchandising campaigns that promote loud deer calls, mostly grunt calls, as the only ones to buy to ensure success. Nothing could be further from the truth. Take a moment to stop and think about it. Most of us have heard the varied low guttural sounds of a buck grunt. Even at its most aggressive levels, it isn't a sound that can be heard by hunters over long distances. Subtler grunt vocalizations made by a buck are even harder to hear, even at close ranges. A buck making a soft grunt can be difficult to hear at just twenty yards.

Once you know all this, it quickly becomes obvious that a grunt call other hunters can hear over two hundred yards away won't sound natural. I don't think there is a hunter out there who has heard a buck in the woods grunting as loudly as a bull. If they did, we'd all be in our stands listening to a crescendo of loud *brp . . . brp . . . brp* sounds reverberating through the woods. It just doesn't happen that way.

So keep your calling soft and subtle most of the time and you will have much more success as a deer caller.

Need further proof? Imagine that you're in your stand and you spot an eight-point buck walking through the woods. You decide to make a loud, aggressive grunt. The buck turns his head, looks in your direction, then swings his head back, drops it slightly, flags his tail twice, and continues on his way. You grunt again, thinking that maybe he didn't hear you or that he just isn't interested in responding. Neither of these two assumptions is correct.

Basically, by grunting too loudly, you've sent the buck an emphatic verbal message that you're a mature, aggressive buck issuing a challenge. Initially, he looks to make eye contact, but he instinctively knows this is a serious mistake. By swinging his head away and dropping it slightly, and then flicking his tail and slowly walking away, he avoids a confrontation with what he perceives to be a more powerful buck. This is the real reason he won't look back or react to the grunt again. All he wants to do at this point is put as much ground between the two of you as possible.

Unfortunately, most hunters interpret the buck's behavior as an apparent lack of interest or presume that he didn't hear the grunt. The hunter's natural response is to grunt again, and in

This buck heard a deep, aggressive grunt that caused him to leave the doe and trot off. The signal he received was that a huge buck was ready to kick his rump unless he cleared out fast. (Ted Rose)

most cases even louder. Now it's the buck's turn to do some interpreting. He instinctively believes that the more aggressive buck is going to pursue him, so he moves away with more determination than ever.

No matter how long or hard you grunt at a buck in this situation, he won't respond to your call. It's only natural that he'd want to get as far away as he can from what he perceives to be the biggest and baddest buck in the woods. Even if this buck is large and heavily antlered, he'll try to avoid a fight with a buck he thinks is even larger and more aggressive than he is.

If you still have doubts about this, think back to all the times you've seen this exact reaction from a buck you were grunting at in a loud and aggressive manner. Trust me, keep your calls soft and you will be more successful.

DON'T OVER-CALL

The next most common reason for a lack of success in calling deer is over-calling. Any turkey hunter can tell you that a gobbler not only hears the seductive calls a hunter is making from up to two hundred yards away, but he also is able to immediately determine exactly where the call is coming from at closer ranges. A savvy, call-shy gobbler then quietly slips in to check out the sounds he is hearing. If the turkey hunter continues to call as the gobbler approaches, he never even realizes that the bird "made" him and is just as quietly sneaking off. The same holds true for a wary buck.

So keep the volume of your calls low, but also make them infrequently enough to not give yourself away. It's always better to build a buck's curiosity with infrequent calls and then let him get frustrated enough to give himself away as he searches for the sounds you made. Use common sense to limit the number of calls you make, whether imitating a competing buck or an estrus doe.

One critical mistake the hunter often makes is to call when a buck has already responded to an earlier call and is walking toward him. Once you see or hear the deer responding, stop calling. Again, let the deer's curiosity work for you instead of against you.

This buck "made" the hunter who was calling to him and took off at top speed. Over-calling often gives the hunter away. (Ted Rose)

PRACTICE

The most important advice I can give you about calling is to practice each call long before the season. Practice not only makes you a better caller, it also enhances your confidence level tremendously. In *Whitetail Strategies*, I wrote, "Concentration + Positive Thinking × Confidence = Consistent Success." And it bears repeating here, because being confident in your ability to imitate different deer sounds and knowing when to use an alarm snort as opposed to a social snort will put antlers on your wall and venison in your freezer.

When you think you've practiced your calling techniques enough, practice, practice, and practice some more.

Ted Rose

Chapter
7

THE SNORT AND
ITS VARIATIONS

The snort is the most often misunderstood primary vocalization. It's often thought of as a sound a deer makes when it's alarmed or running away, so hunters don't use this call very much. That is a real shame, because the primary snort and its four sub-sounds, or cadences, may be the most effective deer vocalization a hunter can make. However, as with any of the vocalizations, a hunter must know when he should blow a particular sub-call or the inevitable result will be a deer streaking away with its tail flying high behind it.

As soon as you decipher what each snort call actually means—or, for that matter, what every cadence of each primary vocalization means—you'll discover how potent this call can be. A snort can be used to stop, relax, attract, and even spook or roust deer from heavy cover. The latter is my favorite way to use the snort sound.

As early as 1988, I decided that the different vocalizations of the snort needed to be given specific names in order for hunters to better differentiate between each call. I labeled the primary

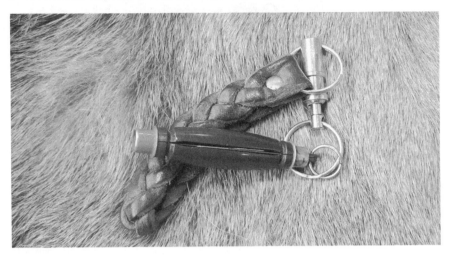

I never go hunting without a snort call like this one from Lohman. (It can be hard to find in stores, but is available on my web site at www.deerdoctor.com.)

snort's four cadences as the alarm snort, the social snort, the alarm-distress snort, and the aggressive snort. Each sound has a distinct meaning to deer.

When the proper snort is used at the right time and under the right set of circumstances, a hunter can trick a buck or doe into thinking he is just another deer. Use the wrong cadence at the wrong time and place, though, and the deer you're calling to will turn itself inside out as it tries to get away.

THE ALARM-DISTRESS SNORT

The alarm-distress is by far my favorite snort cadence. Why? Because its sound forces the deer to react out of instinct. Nothing is better when it comes to hunting a wise old buck. Locate thick cover, like a cedar patch or a swamp, and then post hunters along the networks of trails that are known deer escape routes. Don't let the hunters penetrate too deeply into the center of the cover. After all the standers are posted, wait a good half hour for things to settle down. Then walk into the middle of the thickest part of the cover without worrying about being too quiet. When you've reached the spot where you want to be, take out interdigital scent and lay down several drops. Now stomp your foot several times while blowing the alarm-distress cadence of the primary snort.

The call sounds like this: *Whew . . . whew . . . whew . . . whew, whew, whew, whew.* Make the first three snorts loud and hesitate about a second between each one. Then make the next four snorts quickly, without any hesitation.

It's important to always create as natural a display as possible when calling, or when rattling or decoying. Try to duplicate what deer would do when they're vocalizing, responding to antler rattling, or coming in to check out a decoy.

Make an all-out effort to create all the sounds, smells, and motions (shaking brush or saplings) that deer make when they're calling. All of this helps put a deer at ease when it responds to you. The deer naturally thinks it is hearing, smelling, and sometimes seeing another deer, so it responds more enthusiastically and with less caution.

The alarm-distress is also useful when you're hunting alone, which is when I've had the most success with this cadence of the snort. I use it to roust deer from cattails, ledges, brush piles, small woodlots, laurels, and standing corn. In addition, I've done very well with this call when walking through blowdowns.

Several years ago I was hunting in a place I call the "Honey Hole," a deep bowl surrounded by mountains. It takes a lot of effort and time to reach, which keeps most hunters away. As the hunting season progresses, I find more and more mature bucks using the Honey Hole to escape the pressure in the surrounding valleys and mountains where most hunters post.

I've taken several nicely racked bucks at this location over the years. It's the perfect terrain from which to call or rattle. There is a big swamp in the middle, which is rimmed with large

The snort is one of the most misunderstood of all the deer calls. Learn when and where it should be used and you will see and take more deer.

blowdowns along its edge. I have often seen bucks rise from behind deadfalls in the middle of the day to feed or move away from the area.

On this particular morning I reached the Honey Hole after a two-hour hike, just as large snowflakes began to fall. I took up a position on a side hill and soon spotted a doe that walked behind a large blowdown and disappeared. I studied the area with my binoculars and finally found the doe's face as she lay comfortably under the downed tree, looking back over her shoulder. My gut told me that she was looking at a buck, so I kept watching the area intently.

About twenty minutes later I saw what I thought was one side of a set of antlers. I wasn't sure if my strained eyes were playing tricks on me or if there really was a buck bedded with the doe. I had two options. I could try to outwait them, hoping they'd eventually rise and move. Or I could take a more proactive approach by trying to make something happen without the deer exploding out of the cover and running off before I could get a shot.

I decided the best strategy would be to blow an alarm-distress call. I put out several drops of interdigital gland scent, and from behind a large oak I stomped my foot several times and blew the alarm-distress: *Whew . . . whew . . . whew . . . whew, whew, whew, whew.*

Within seconds, the doe stood up and began to intently scan the area to find out what caused the other "deer" to blow an alarm-distress cadence. While she was swinging her head from side to side, the buck stood up. I could see instantly that he was a keeper. Not wanting to take any chances by waiting around, the buck scaled the big blowdown, sniffed the air, and was about to take off in another direction when the report from my Ruger .44

The alarm-distress call has provided me many shot opportunities at bucks and does bedded in the safety of blowdowns. Their instinctive response to this call gave their locations away.

Mag echoed off the surrounding mountains. (I always use my lightweight Ruger in areas that require long walks up and down mountains and through thick cover, especially when a quick second shot may be necessary.)

Without the alarm-distress call, I seriously doubt I'd have ever gotten a chance at this buck. The snow was already falling hard, and trying to wait him out would have probably been the wrong tactic. By using a cadence I knew would pull the deer from cover, I created a shot opportunity I otherwise wouldn't have had.

I've used this call to roust bucks out of small patches of cover on farms, in swales, and even in heavy thorn brush. Most hunters walk by this type of cover, thinking the undergrowth is either too small to harbor a buck or too impenetrable to check out.

A small buck I shot in the early 1970s offers a classic example. I was hunting on a farm we called "Weissmans." As I walked across an open field, I passed a thick patch of overgrown brush I had probably walked by a hundred times before. As I looked at it this time I thought to myself, I wonder how many times I've walked past a deer bedded in there.

I flung a heavy branch into the thicket. Nothing happened. So I took my snort call out and blew the alarm-distress. I was still learning the nuances of calling back then, which meant that I wasn't using interdigital scent and I wasn't stomping my foot to create the full illusion. I just blew the alarm-distress a few times.

I hadn't even finished the second sequence when a small buck broke from the cover and started running across the field. I dropped him just before he reached the bordering woodlot. Even though I suspected the call might work, it was still early enough in my trial-and-error days that I was totally shocked to see it actually do the job it was supposed to do. The young buck reacted predictably and immediately to what it perceived to be a serious problem.

Leo Somma paused to blow an alarm-distress call while walking through some thick blowdowns. This buck stood up long enough for him to get a clear shot.

Again, I never would have had the opportunity to shoot this buck if I hadn't used the alarm-distress to force him out.

Remember, this call works so well because all deer learned from the time they were old enough to run that this particular cadence of the snort requires an instant flee response. It is ingrained in their heads as a natural behavior.

Blowing the alarm-distress snort has created numerous shot opportunities for me through the years. Without it, many a buck would have remained safely hidden within sanctuaries of thick cover.

THE ALARM SNORT

The alarm cadence of the primary snort is the most recognized vocalization deer make. I can even tell you when and where hunters probably encounter a deer making this snort. Often, a

Here Leo is drawing a bead on a buck he rousted from a patch of standing corn with an alarm-distress snort.

hunter jumps a deer while walking along a logging road or making his way through the woods to his stand. Because the deer doesn't see or wind the hunter first, it reacts only to the noise the hunter is making. If it had winded or sighted the hunter, it would have quietly snuck off or blown the alarm-distress call as it made a hasty retreat.

But this deer is confused, so it blows the alarm call. It doesn't really know what spooked it, and it often remains standing or slowly walks a short distance and blows the call again. This call is a specific noise. Every hunter has heard this snort often. And the deer that makes this call can be easily called back if you know exactly what to do.

When you encounter a deer unexpectedly, the deer may respond by blowing a single snort, and then running several yards before stopping and blowing a second single snort: *whew . . . whew.* It's alarmed, but it hasn't been able to pinpoint why. It knows instinctively that it's safer not to run any farther until it can determine exactly what made it nervous.

This is the point at which you either make or break your opportunity to call the deer back. I've learned through trial and error to stop in my tracks as soon as the deer sounds the alarm. I immediately blow a single snort back at the deer. Be careful here, though. If the sound you heard appears to be fifty yards or closer, one single snort is all you can risk without being discovered by the deer. If you estimate the range at over fifty yards you can make two single snorts: a snort, a brief second or two of silence, and then another single snort: *whew . . .   . . . whew.*

The deer is trying to locate and isolate the danger. By blowing back at the deer with the alarm cadence of the primary snort call, you stimulate its curiosity. Often, after hearing what it perceives to be just a call from another deer, it decides to slowly make its way back toward the location where it first perceived the danger.

As long as the deer remains at a distance and continues to blow one or two snorts, you can keep blowing a single snort. Continue to do this unless the deer begins to walk toward you. The instant the deer moves in your direction, stop calling. Even if the deer continues to snort at this point, you must remain silent to let its curiosity build. This is your best chance at pulling the deer within shooting distance.

Years ago, my wife shot her first buck while still-hunting toward her tree stand. She spotted a deer, but as she tried to position herself for a shot she stepped on a branch. The deer heard the snap and blew an alarm snort. True to form, it ran off several yards and then blew a second snort. Kate blew back at the deer and the buck answered.

Each time the deer answered, it blew two snorts but didn't move. And each time Kate blew back two snorts. The buck, curious to see what had frightened it, finally came closer with each series of alarm snorts. After several minutes of exchanging snorts, the spike buck made its last move, stepping out from behind the cedars where Kate dispatched him with one clean shot. She would never have had the chance to shoot that buck if she hadn't known how to call back an alarmed deer.

I also use the alarm snort to help roust deer from cover when I'm still-hunting with my bow. I intentionally walk through heavy cover with the wind in my face. Every few steps I snap a twig or kick some leaves, hoping the noise will alarm a buck. Once I make contact with a buck and he makes the alarm snort, I know I have a better than average chance of calling him back.

I often refer to the alarm snort as my "too late" call. Too late for the buck, that is. As the buck and I exchange calls, he usually approaches without knowing I'm hidden in heavy brush or pines, and he continues to walk by me in search of the other "deer." I've shot a few nice bucks at distances less than ten yards while using the alarm snort. Again, the trick is to stop calling when the buck closes to within fifty yards or less. This heightens the curiosity of the buck, drawing it all the way in for the shot.

While all variations of the snort work well, you'll find that the alarm snort is the easiest call to master. Keep in mind, however, that a critical aspect when using a snort call is to not blow an alarm snort to a deer who is vocalizing an alarm-distress snort. You must recognize the different cadences of each call to use them effectively.

I shot this buck in western New York while still-hunting through a recently logged woodlot. He was bedded behind a tangle of brush but rose to the sounds of my calling.

THE SOCIAL SNORT

The social snort is usually made by a nervous deer warily feeding at the edge of a field or in a woodlot. I'm sure you've seen and heard a deer make this call.

The animal puts its head down to feed while focusing its ears in a particular direction. It then lifts its head quickly, looking in the direction its ears were pointing. Reluctantly, the deer lowers its head to begin feeding again, only to repeat the process. This nervous behavior goes on for several minutes before the deer decides to blow a single non-aggressive snort. By blowing the snort, the deer is trying to encourage whatever is making it nervous to reveal itself by approaching it, or at least answering. If it's reacting to another deer nearby, that deer will often answer with a single snort of its own.

This return call immediately relaxes the first deer, which then begins to feed more contentedly, without lifting its head every few seconds. Often the deer feeds in the direction of the deer that answered it—safety in numbers. If it doesn't hear a return social snort after making one, the deer usually stops feeding and retreats from the area.

When I see a deer acting like this, I know I can relax it and sometimes even attract it to me by using the social cadence of the primary snort. But it's important to remember that the social snort only works on deer that are exhibiting the type of behavior described above.

Never make this call unless the deer first makes a single quick snort. When it drops its head back down to feed, make one soft snort to the deer. Try to blow the call in the opposite direction of the deer. If the call is made correctly, the deer typically lifts its head, cups its ears toward you, and then begins to feed again, many times heading in your direction. If the deer lifts its head and becomes even more nervous, you probably blew the call too loudly. Don't try to make another call until the deer starts to feed again.

I used the social snort to attract a good eight-point buck once while bowhunting in Hope, New Jersey. The buck was nervously feeding on acorns in a small woodlot that bordered an agricultural field. Every few seconds he perked up his ears and looked behind him. Then he put his nose into the leaves and resumed the search for more acorns.

Before long, the buck's ears started playing the radar game again. He lifted his head, stared into a thicket, and walked off a short distance in the opposite direction of the bushes. I noticed that he was getting more and more spooked with each passing minute, and that he was moving away from my stand.

I waited until the buck put his head down to feed again, and then I turned away from him and softly blew a single snort. The buck lifted its head, stared in my direction, and then began to feed again. Only this time, he moved purposefully and steadily toward me while feeding.

I knew enough to stop calling at this point, letting the deer dictate my next move. Within two minutes of my first snort, the buck was under my tree stand. I released my arrow as the buck's nose was buried in the leaves looking for acorns. He never suspected a thing.

If I hadn't relaxed the buck with a social snort, I doubt a shot opportunity would have presented itself. I think the buck would have eventually become too nervous from the original noise, moving out of bow range and maybe even out of the area entirely. This encounter may have come to nothing if I'd lacked the understanding and confidence to make a social snort.

Knowing when, how, why, and where to use this cadence has been crucial to my success.

THE AGGRESSIVE SNORT

The aggressive snort is the fourth cadence of the primary snort. This is sometimes referred to as the grunt-snort-wheeze. But this isn't correct. A buck that is annoyed and trying to establish itself within the social pecking order makes the aggressive snort. This is a loud and overblown call, meant to get the attention of another, offending deer. It's often made so powerfully that the deer expels air and mucus from its nostrils.

Does make this call to fawns, yearlings, and other competing does when food sources are scarce. The call is also associated with an action known as "flailing," which occurs when a deer rises on its hind legs and strikes at the head or body of another deer with its forelegs.

All deer that are lower on the totem pole than the deer making this vocalization pay attention to it instantly. These submissive deer quickly move off several feet from the more aggressive deer.

Mature bucks regularly vocalize to lesser bucks with this type of snort. They use it to let them know they are about to convert their antagonism from a simple call to a greater physical confrontation. It is most often used by bucks during the three phases of the rut. A younger satellite buck typically hangs close to an estrus doe with a mature buck in the hopes of getting into the action. Many times, when all other body language fails to dissuade the youngster, the mature buck blows an aggressive snort. It's a warning to the smaller buck to back off or deal with the consequences.

Normally, this cadence of the snort scares more bucks than it attracts. But there is a time when it can be used to attract a buck. If you encounter a situation like the one I described above, wait until the mature buck blows the aggressive snort and then make an aggressive snort of your own in his direction. The message you're sending is that you're a competing mature buck of his age-class and rank in the pecking order. The call is telling him you aren't afraid of his warning and, in fact, are daring to challenge him for the doe he is tending.

In all the years I've used this call, I've noted only two types of reaction. Either a buck immediately uses his antlers to prod the doe to

An aggressive snort call helped Jay Cassell lure this monster within range.

retreat to another area, thereby leaving the "challenging buck" in the dust, or depending on his mood, he stiff-legs his way toward the challenger with his ears laid back, nostrils flared, and the hair on his neck standing up. All of this happens while he blows aggressive snorts. It is a visual and vocal demonstration that he is big enough and strong enough to not be intimidated by any other buck in the area.

Using the aggressive snort is always a gamble. You quickly lose the buck or get him to respond. But I think it's better to have a 50-50 chance to get the buck rather than to helplessly watch him walk off.

This is a neat call to master. And while it may not attract a lot of bucks, when it does it'll be an experience you'll always remember.

To do the aggressive snort call correctly, you have to break my cardinal rule about calling softly—just this one time. After hearing the buck or doe make this call, muster up all the lung power you can and blow two hard snorts back-to-back—*Whew, Whew*—and then wait. If the deer moves toward you, don't make another call. If he moves away and continues to blow an aggressive snort while doing so, you can also blow an aggressive snort until the buck responds or moves off entirely.

The wise hunter never assumes that a buck that doesn't initially respond, or one that moves off into heavy cover, has decided not to respond at all. Sometimes, the aggressive snort is nothing more than a bluff, even when the deer is a mature buck. He heads to cover only to cautiously circle the challenging buck in an attempt to catch him by surprise.

When I blow an aggressive snort to a buck and he moves off into the woods, I wait a good hour before giving up on him. Heed my advice: Watch the surrounding cover and listen carefully for a good hour. The buck may be circling with the wind in his nose, looking to sneak up on the interloper. This is a good time to be off the ground!

Chapter
8

BLEATS AND BLATS AND THEIR VARIATIONS

The four primary vocalizations deer make include the blat and the bleat. All deer younger than eighteen months old— yearlings and fawns—generally make bleats, while all adult deer make blats. There is a significant difference in the sound of each of these calls. Any seasoned turkey hunter will tell you the same thing is true with this species. The sounds of an adult boss gobbler or hen are markedly different from those of a poult or jake.

It's important to note that some manufacturers who make deer calls refer to both the fawn and adult sounds as bleats. And some companies identify the adult sound as an "adult bleat." To keep from getting confused, keep in mind that any package labeled "adult bleat" really just means "blat." If you're looking for a fawn bleat, make sure the package is marked as a fawn or yearling call.

If you have trouble locating the correct blat or bleat call, visit my web site, www.deerdoctor.com, where you can purchase either type. Or you can e- mail me with any questions you have about using these calls at peter@fiduccia.com.

Don't confuse bleat and blat calls, which are made by deer of different age-classes. Here, I'm using an adult blat call.

FAWN BLEATS

Because fawn bleat calls are most productive from September through the end of October, they're primarily helpful for the early season bowhunter. When made correctly and used at the right time, these calls can be lethal.

Fawns make several variations of a bleat. They bleat when they're hungry, lost, hurt, in immediate danger, frightened, or simply when they want attention. Each sound is broken down into the following categories: the locating bleat, the alarm-distress bleat, the social bleat, and the feeding bleat.

THE LOCATING BLEAT

A fawn that is unexpectedly separated from its group will make a whining bleat over and over again in an attempt to locate the doe or another deer (once the danger has passed). This is one of the easiest fawn bleats to imitate, and it's also one of the more effective calls.

Unlike the way she responds to the alarm-distress sound of a fawn, a doe doesn't respond to the locating bleat with much urgency. Instead, she calmly makes her way toward the area the sound is coming from in an attempt to locate the lost fawn or yearling. The entire family group often follows her, including any young bucks that are still with the group. At other times, mature bucks hear this sound and respond instinctively, knowing that a doe must be close by.

Whenever I see a fawn separated from the group, I immediately make the locating bleat. Sometimes the doe stops in her tracks and slowly makes her way back. Other times, bucks appear out of nowhere in response to the sound.

THE ALARM-DISTRESS BLEAT

When the doe hears the alarm-distress bleat made by a yearling, or especially a fawn, it only takes her moments to respond. As she urgently makes her way toward the sound, the rest of her group

Several companies make blat and bleat cans, but I think the Primos can calls make the most realistic sounds.

will again instinctively follow in most instances. As I noted above, this group frequently includes a yearling buck or two. A mature buck may occasionally respond since he's likely to locate a doe near the source of the distress call, but he usually does so with caution because the sound means the fawn is in danger.

My newest DVD, *Tactics for "Talking" to Deer*, includes footage of does being called in with the alarm-distress call. The does react immediately, racing in to rescue the fawn or yearling they think is in trouble. The response to this call can be so dramatic that it often catches the hunter off-guard.

My new DVD on calling covers all four primary sounds—the grunt, blat, bleat, and snort—and their variations. I explain how, when, why, and where to use them most effectively.

Once you blow this call, you must be ready for action. No other sound prompts deer, especially does, to respond so quickly. This can be one of the most fun calls to use. There have been times when I haven't been able to draw back my bow or make the shot because I'm laughing so hard at the response of the doe.

THE SOCIAL BLEAT

The social bleat is a sound regularly made by yearlings and fawns as a greeting call. It is a soft sound, barely audible to humans, but deer hear it easily. Youngsters usually make it as one group moves into an area with other deer. It is meant to be a relaxing call or an introductory sound to the other deer. I use it when I see a group of deer passing my stand and I want to stop them to get a shot or to see if there is a buck following them.

THE FEEDING BLEAT

A fawn that wants to be fed, which may still happen as late as September or October, will make a long, whiney bleat over and over again until the doe responds. During September, this neonatal sound still plays heavily on the doe's maternal instincts, and she will usually respond to it. In October, however, she is less inclined to feed the fawn because by this time she wants it to be permanently weaned off her milk. But even then it's hard for her to ignore her maternal duties, and most times she eventually seeks out the source of the sound. I don't use this call at all after October, as it is rarely effective.

THE ADULT BLAT

All adult deer—over 1½ years old—make the loud blat. It is the most common vocalization among all deer in the woods. The blat is used in a variety of cadences to locate, warn, fend off, attract, and generally communicate. Because it's the primary sound used by all deer, it arouses the curiosity of both bucks and does without question. As with the bleat, hunters will benefit from recognizing some of the most common blat variations.

THE SOCIAL BLAT

The social blat is used when deer communicate with one another under non-pressured, casual circumstances. This sound—*Baa-Baaaaaa . . . Baa-baaaaaa*—should be blown gently. Stretch it out to a whine at the end of the call, and do not blow the call

Markus Wilhelm, President of Outdoorsman's Edge Book Club, poses with a hefty ten-point buck I called in from over two hundred yards away using a social blat.

often. Once every thirty to forty-five minutes is enough. If a deer approaches, stop calling. This spurs the deer to intensify its search for the source.

Just like yearlings and fawns use the bleat, adult deer make the social call as they approach other deer. Does also make it when they approach a buck. It is a relaxing sound to deer and will calm the nerves of spooky whitetails. I use it to keep nervous does from leaving my area, especially during the rut.

My long-time adage, "If you want to kill a buck, hunt the does," should be taken to heart. While bucks can be elusive most of the time, they are on the hunt for does during the chase period of the rut and during the rut itself. By keeping does in sight during these periods, you automatically up your chances of seeing and bagging a buck.

It isn't widely known that mule deer, especially bucks, respond readily to adult blats. This buck came in within minutes of my call.

THE ALARM BLAT

This is one of the most useful calls you can make to stop deer dead in their tracks. I don't care how fast a deer is running, when it hears an alarm blat it skids to a halt to discover where it came from.

This is one of the few calls that I recommend blowing loudly. If you see a buck making his way past your stand and he's moving too fast to get a bead on, just blow a single loud alarm blat: *Baa-Baaaaaaaaaaaa*. I can almost guarantee you that the deer will slide to a stop in order to determine why another deer is blowing an alarm. It doesn't want to move in a direction that would put it in harm's way, so it stops to get its bearings.

Sometimes a deer will only stop for a few seconds before moving off again. Other times, a deer will remain motionless for several

Stopping a monster buck like this, especially when he is chasing a hot doe, shouldn't be left to chance. Whistling may or may not work, but an alarm blat will always stop him in his tracks for at least a few seconds. (Ted Rose)

minutes. In either case, the hunter now has time to make a shot on an animal that was running too fast for a clean, accurate kill.

Many hunters have told me they simply whistle at running deer to make them stop. While this tactic does work on occasion, my experience has been that whistling is more likely to send a running deer into warp drive. Trust me, correctly blowing an alarm blat with your mouth or with a call will stop a deer in its tracks every time.

I suggest learning to make this call, and all the adult blats, for that matter, with your mouth. This is easy to do. Simply tuck in your chin and make a deep, lamb-like sound: *Baaaaaaaaaaaaaa*. In fact, it's not difficult to mimic each of the adult blats with your mouth. The more you practice, the better you will get. Before you know it, you'll be able to make all variations of the blat with your mouth just as effectively as any manufactured call.

This call is also excellent for hunters who shoot long distances. I used an alarm blat in Wyoming years ago while taping one of my *Woods N' Water* TV segments. There were three mature bucks on a ridgetop about three hundred yards away. They were slowly walking from right to left along the ridgeline. My rifle was wedged in the fork of a tree and I made a loud blat (louder than normal because of the distance). All three bucks immediately stopped and stared down in the direction of the call.

I placed my crosshairs on the middle buck because he was the largest. While the three bucks stood there motionless, I had plenty of time to figure the wind direction and distance. I then took my shot. I heard the bullet smack the deer, and we watched the buck drop like a lead weight between the other two. As the remaining bucks ran off, I blew another alarm blat, again stopping them cold. This was quite a testament to the effectiveness of the call.

I have stopped and taken many deer since then with the alarm blat. Last year, while hunting on my farm in New York, I jumped a small buck that bolted off through the woods. I made an alarm blat with my mouth, and he stopped about sixty yards from where I'd jumped him. I quickly put the scope on him, only to discover he was a seven-point. I passed on the shot because part of our management policy on the farm is to not take any bucks with fewer than eight points or with racks less than eighteen inches wide.

Anyone who wants to improve his shot opportunities by bringing deer to a standstill needs to learn this call.

THE ESTRUS-DOE BLAT

One of my favorite calls during any of the three phases of the rut is the estrus-doe blat. I find it extremely effective from mid-December through late January during the late, or post, rut. This is a time when a lot of yearlings and fawns come into their first or second heat. Since most adult does have already been bred, these hot younger does are absolute magnets for bucks.

It isn't unusual to see a single doe being followed by more than one mature buck during this period. Countless times over the years I've seen several bucks on the trail of one hot doe over the course of a few hours. The estrus-doe blat will work magic on any buck following the trail of one of these hot young does.

Another advantage to using the estrus blat occurs when a buck hangs up after you've rattled or grunted to it. Too many hunters get stuck in the mindset that the only call that will attract a big mature buck during the rut is the grunt. If you want to increase your success hunting bucks by at least 50 percent, learn to make an estrus-doe blat.

Find an area that does use frequently. During the rut, an estrus doe walks through the woods emitting these blats to attract bucks that haven't yet picked up her scent.

My neighbor used an estrus-doe bleat to stop this terrific ten-point buck as it walked past his stand.

Blow the call with reasonable volume—but not too loud—to create a drawn-out *Baaaaaaaah . . . Baaaaaaaah*. Repeat this call two or three times and then stop. Wait about fifteen minutes and then make another two or three calls. Repeat this sequence for up to an hour. After that, it has been my experience that waiting an additional hour to make the calls again is more beneficial than continuing to blow regularly.

This call brings bucks in from long distances. Sometimes a buck even runs right in. But most times they respond cautiously, even though they come in quickly. Once again, the key to success is to stop calling the moment you see or hear any kind of response. Let the buck's curiosity build enough that he continues to search frantically for what he believes is a hot doe.

This is the one call I can depend on to pull in deer that are hung up in cover, and it's a terrific late-season deer vocalization that has attracted big bucks for me in many different states.

Because deer move about much more during the midday hours late in the season, I strongly recommend hunting the "off hours" between 10:30 AM and 1:30 PM. In fact, if you follow only one recommendation from this book, make it this one.

In order to consistently kill mature whitetail bucks, you must believe from the bottom of your heart that big bucks don't go totally nocturnal. Take that to the deer hunting bank. Big bucks become extremely sensitive to your scent and pressure, no matter how slight. It only takes a few days of a hunter scouting or walking its home area before a buck knows that something has changed and that the hunt has begun.

As soon as he figures this out, he adjusts his movement patterns accordingly. He understands instinctively that between the morning hours of 6:00 and 9:30 his home range is being invaded by hunters. He has lived ten months of the year without such pressure, and even the dumbest of bucks is able to react to this kind of unusual activity.

These bucks get the same message from about 2 PM to dark. Common sense tells you what options are left for the buck. If he is interested in feeding or looking for does, nothing short of hunting pressure or human scent stops him from getting up during the midday hours and moving out. He may not move far, but trust me, he will move.

If you truly believe that all mature bucks "go nocturnal," at some point you have to wonder how big bucks still manage to get shot during daylight hours.

When you're hunting the midday, or off, hours try not to stay in one stand all day. You won't be hunting as effectively as possible. Your scent will permeate the area and you will eventually become distracted enough to miss things. If you want to stay in the woods all day, try the following. Hunt one stand from daylight to 9:30 AM, and then move to another stand a few hundred yards away from 10:30 AM to 1:30 PM. Finally, return to your original stand from 2 to 5 PM.

Chances are, you won't need to return to your evening stand. I have taken 60 percent of all my mature bucks between 10:30 AM and 1:30 PM. In fact, on many occasions I've gone out only during the off-hours, especially in extremely cold weather, and still bagged a mature buck.

By the way, because November through January can be cold, particularly in the northern states, protect your blat call from freezing—assuming you're using a commercial call—by placing it inside the breast pocket of your shirt underneath your jacket.

One of the most dramatic examples of the usefulness of an estrus-doe blat call occurred on a I hunt I had in Canada. It was a colder than normal morning, even for northern Saskatchewan. A doe broke from the woodlot about 150 yards from my stand and quickly ran fifty yards or so into an open field. She only paused for a moment before darting just as quickly back into the woods. She repeated this routine several more times during the next ten minutes. Each time she entered the field she made several short, loud blats and then dashed back into the woods.

I quickly realized this doe was in peak estrus, and the odds were great that a buck was hovering in the cover of the woods near the edge of the field.

The next time she ran into the field, I made several short estrus blats. Instead of running back to the woods, she nervously trotted along the wood line toward me. Moments later, she was below my stand, trying to locate what she thought was a competing estrus doe. Ignoring her, I focused my concentration on the woods, searching for her would-be suitor.

It didn't take long for me to see parts of a buck as he steadily but cautiously moved through the trees toward the doe. I heard his soft guttural grunts and the sounds of leaves crunching and twigs snapping as he got closer and closer to the stand. He was moving quickly enough that I couldn't risk taking a shot at him.

When he got within fifty yards of my stand, I blew one soft blat. The sound made the doe run a dozen or more feet closer to me, blatting as she came. The buck stood motionless at this point. I raised my rifle and quickly scanned his ten-point rack. Without a doubt, he was a keeper.

I flipped the safety off the Ruger and was about to fire when a slight movement behind the buck caught my attention. At first I thought I was seeing a large heavy branch moving in the background, but then I saw an eye and an ear. I quickly put the crosshairs on the spot and saw a huge-racked buck. Without counting points, I instinctively knew I should shoot him.

This all took place in a matter of seconds, although it felt like several minutes. Before I could settle the crosshairs on a vital area of the buck, the doe reacted to my movement, despite how carefully I was trying to avoid alerting her. With a leap, both bucks disappeared into the woods.

I spent the next hour trying to call the doe back without success. The temperature was minus 30 degrees, and it was way too cold to remain on stand. In fact, my wife, who is also my long-time cameraperson when she isn't in front of the camera hunting or cooking, whispered to me, "Actually, in a way it's a blessing that they ran off. It's so cold the camera isn't operational—it's frozen!"

It took five long, very cold days, but on the last day of the hunt I called in another doe from another location using an estrus blat. She trotted from the woods and ran across an open field and past my stand, looking for the competing doe. Moments later, the huge buck broke from cover and chased after her.

I shot him as he reached the end of the field. Unfortunately, I hit him farther back than I'd intended, and he swerved hard and ran into the woods below me. I thought I'd missed him because he didn't show any reaction to being hit. But I did hear the bullet smack into something, so we checked the video and it was clear that I hit the buck in a vital area, albeit behind where I was aiming.

When I reached the hit site I discovered dark-brown and grayish hair with black tips, a strong indication that I had hit him in the liver or kidney area. I immediately realized that even as excited as I was, I had to give him at least thirty minutes before following his blood trail. The dark-red, almost maroon, blood was another indication that I'd hit the liver or kidney. Hits in this area bleed profusely, so the trail was easy to follow.

I waited the half hour and then took up the trail. After following it for a couple hundred yards, I noticed the buck bedded down in heavy cover. He strained to get to his feet and wobbled as he stood. A second shot to the neck ended the hunt.

The buck turned out to be an atypical sixteen-point with a rack that had mass from burr to antler tip. His green score was 207 1/8, with a net Boone & Crockett score of 195 3/8.

The fact that this buck is now in my trophy room all boiled down to knowing when, where, how, and why to use an estrus-doe

One soft blat call brought me this sixteen-point Saskatchewan buck, my biggest to date.

blat. Hunters should be aware that an estrus blat can often be more successful in calling in wary bucks and does than a grunt call. This even applies to bucks that hang up when called to with a grunt. I've learned through experience that during the chase period of the primary rut, it's better to call to hot estrus does than it is to try attracting a buck with a grunt call. (See chapter 10 for further details on this aspect of the rut.)

Once you attract a doe, it doesn't matter how big or wary a buck is; she will lead him to your stand as neatly as if he had a ring through his nose.

Chapter
9

THE GRUNT AND
ITS VARIATIONS

The grunt call, along with every other deer call, works best when you let the deer's curiosity work for you instead of against you. Let a buck's inquisitiveness build to a fever pitch, until he can't stand it anymore and brazenly walks out into the open to locate the source of the call. You can make grunt calls throughout the day. During firearm season, however, don't grunt during prime times (i.e., from dawn to 9:00 AM and from 2:00 PM to dusk, when a majority of other hunters are in the woods). Instead, grunt between the midday hours of 10:00 AM and 2:00 PM. Your score rate will rise dramatically.

Many hunters have told me that they've only had mixed success with grunt calls. Sometimes they attract bucks, and sometimes they don't. Invariably, they want to know why. Well, there are many reasons why grunts and other calls work well at some times but not others. Most times, though, a negative response is generated after a grunt is blown too loudly and aggressively.

Imagine that an eight-point buck of average size is walking up a trail with his nose held to the ground. Suddenly he hears your loud, aggressive grunt. In deer language what you've just done is yell "Hey you!" at the top of your lungs. You just scared the crap out of the poor buck.

What happens next is automatic. Out of instinct, he glances in your direction and then realizes he made a critical mistake by attempting to make eye contact with a more aggressive animal. He avoids a confrontation by immediately looking away and continuing to walk without looking back. No matter how long or

Even though this buck is large, an aggressive grunt call will cause him to move off into cover. He wants nothing to do with what he believes is a more aggressive challenger. (Ted Rose)

hard you grunt at a buck under these conditions, he will not respond. Why should he? With your loud and aggressive call, you just announced that you're unquestionably the biggest, toughest buck in the woods. If this buck has any sense at all, even if he's a large buck, he'll avoid the fight and walk off. Call softly and you'll be more successful.

Along with the snort, the buck grunt is probably the most common vocalization hunters hear in the woods. Though it isn't commonly known, both does and bucks grunt. Does grunt most of the year, and bucks grunt during the rut, but grunting also occurs throughout the year. Grunting like a buck in rut or a doe in estrus works well. The best response to grunting comes between late October and mid-November and again in mid-December. Grunting reaches its peak when both bucks and does are chasing each other or freshening scrapes during the peak rut.

For a grunt call to work effectively, it should be blown gently. If not, you'll scare off more bucks than you'll attract. Even trophy-sized bucks sometimes avoid a conflict when hot on the trail of a doe. Smaller bucks are definitely intimidated by deep guttural grunts. Most hunters liken the grunts they've heard to the sounds made by a domestic pig. Others claim they sound like a burp. Both interpretations are correct.

Other cadences or categories of grunts include the tending grunt, social grunt, submissive grunt, and trail grunt. Still other grunts are combined with snorts and wheezes and are antagonistic to other deer, especially bucks. Deer combine these aggressive grunts with postural threats. Keep in mind that most sexual grunts are short, have a low pitch and intensity, and are repeated only when the deer feels totally secure.

As most hunters know, the grunt call is particularly effective during the rut. But don't confuse actual mating with chasing.

To increase your success rate, keep your grunt calls low and short. (Kate Fiduccia)

Once a buck is paired up with a doe, it's difficult to make him respond; just as it is with any male animal you're trying to call away from a female. Yet, when bucks are chasing after does, grunting can lead to more action than you ever imagined, and sometimes more than you can handle.

I'll cover the rut in more detail in the next chapter, but first let's look at how grunt calls can be used during the rut phases.

GRUNTING DURING THE PRE-RUT

The most overlooked rut stage by hunters is the productive pre-rut. This false rut typically occurs in early October. Archers and firearm sportsmen who hunt during this most beautiful month of the year often find a mass of fresh scrapes throughout their hunting grounds, all made within a twenty-four-hour period. What happens to cause this obvious intense breeding change in bucks? The onset of the pre-rut.

Bucks and does are sexually excited for the first time in many months. They enthusiastically respond to anything that remotely suggests a sexual encounter. This is why false scrapes work so well during the pre-rut and why non-aggressive rattling techniques also get results.

Grunting tactics for the pre-rut are varied. One of the best calls to make at this time is called a trail grunt. I have nicknamed it the "burp-o-matic" or "burp" grunt. It's a series—usually several in succession—of very soft, short, burp-like sounds made by a

Kate shot this buck just as the pre-rut was ending and the big chase phase was about to start. The young buck responded immediately to a soft trail grunt.

buck. Usually his nose is held to the ground and he zigzags along searching out the scent of a doe. This scent doesn't necessarily have to be that of an estrus doe.

Believe it or not, most bucks on these trails are chasing does that are about to enter estrus but haven't yet, which is why they're so excited. Bucks sense that if they can catch up with the doe, they can stay with her until she comes into estrus, when their amorous overtures will be accepted.

Paul Butski is an expert wildlife caller. He has won several national turkey calling championships and now manufactures his own line of game calls. His favorite and most successful deer call is the grunt. "Before I began using the grunt call, I knew bucks were slipping by me undetected. Now, since I've been using the grunt, bucks are coming in and looking for me," said Butski.

To increase your success when grunting, create more of an illusion by combining your grunt with intermittent antler rattling. Also, shake a sapling or the branch of a tree a few times when you're grunting. These sound effects add realism to your grunting.

The most crucial factor to remember about calling is that when a deer responds it is zeroing in directly on the location from which the sound is emanating—that means you. All the deer's senses are focused on the noise. If you continue to call as the deer approaches, you almost guarantee that the deer will "make" you. And when he does, he'll either walk by like you weren't even there or he'll bolt out of there. Sometimes, he'll "make" you from cover some distance away, and you'll never even know he was there.

CALLING IN THE PRIMARY RUT

The primary rut encompasses most of the serious, aggressive behavior of deer during the breeding season. I like to use two different cadences of the grunt during this period. The first is the grunt-snort-wheeze. The second is a variation of the burp grunt discussed above for the pre-rut. The number of burps is reduced and the sounds lengthened.

The grunt-snort-wheeze is an antagonistic, aggressive call. It is the most difficult of all the grunt cadences to master. Bucks of high rank in the herd make this call, and it's meant to get the attention of subordinate bucks. It basically says, "Hey! Do you see this head gear? Are you ready and able to take me on? If not, beat it." And the latter is exactly what most bucks choose when they hear this call from a hunter. But an aggressive buck that holds a high position within the herd is instinctively motivated to respond. I use the grunt-snort-wheeze mostly with aggressive rattling and grunting tactics, which I turn to infrequently.

Begin the call by making a long deep guttural grunt, *Eeeer rrrrp*. Follow this with a short snort, *Whew*. Although this part of the call has always been called a snort, it's more of a nostril-clearing sound than a full-on snort. Imagine you have a runny nose that isn't completely plugged with mucus. If you were to blow your nose hard, you would only hear a quick *whew* sound rather than a long and voluminous mucus-clearing noise.

The final element of this call is a short wheezing sound. This wheezing can best be described as a short cough from deep within the lungs. Just be sure to keep it short. Cough as softly as you can while expelling all the air from your lungs.

Combine these three sounds to create the grunt-snort-wheeze. Don't be disappointed if a buck fails to respond right away, or at all. Again, this call is designed for trophy hunters calling to big bucks that rank high in the pecking order.

The second cadence I use during the primary rut is the extended burp grunt. Some hunters refer to it as the tending grunt. It is usually made by a buck that has an estrus doe feeding or bedded down nearby or, in some instances, an estrus doe that has

While hunting whitetails in Montana, I replied to a grunt-snort-wheeze made by a buck in cover. When I blew the call back, I was surprised to see this muley walk out. Obviously, both mule deer and whitetails respond well to this call.

momentarily walked out of his sightline. The buck grunts every so often to remind the doe of his presence until she's actually ready to breed. He'll also make an extended burp grunt to warn off other bucks.

It is a highly effective call during the primary rut, usually from around November 1 until late December. While this call is a pitch higher than the pre-rut burp grunt, it still isn't made loudly. Every twenty minutes or so, cup the end of the call tube in your palm (the hand should be half-open, not tightly closed) and blow two or three short calls. They sound like this: *Burp, burp, burp.* Each burp is drawn out slightly longer than the pre-rut burp.

When you get a response, whether by sight or sound, immediately stop calling. Deer are edgy after several weeks of hunting pressure, and they react more cautiously to everything, including other deer vocalizations. They often hesitate in the cover, listening and looking before showing themselves. It's a recurring theme throughout this book, but I can't stress enough that it's the deer's curiosity that draws it in for the shot. If you keep blowing on the call after you get a response, the deer will either spot you or be put off. If you sit tight at this point, his inquisitiveness will usually get the better of him.

CALLING POST RUT

During the late rut, most of the immature (latest born) does, and any other does that weren't successfully bred, come into estrus. Many hunters have told me that they've had a lot of success grunting during the late rut. This doesn't surprise me. Grunting can be effective well past the turn of the year because some does are still experiencing estrus cycles in December, January, and even early February. Yet the post rut is a period overlooked by many hunters who are sure that the rut is long over.

Former baseball great Wade Boggs with a handsome ten-point buck that was grunted in during the late rut. (Kate Fiduccia)

One sign to look for during this phase is a quick and dramatic increase in deer activity. Does coming into estrus during this period are particularly attractive to bucks because there aren't many of them and because they tend to have an intensity about their odor and body language.

The does are as bent on finding bucks as the bucks are on finding them. They trot along depositing estrus urine and making a series of soft, prolonged grunts. Although it's the same grunt does make starting back in October, they are more vocal during the post rut.

It's worthwhile to note that the doe grunt is a highly effective call for attracting bucks in any of the rut periods mentioned above. This is especially true during slow periods when bucks are less enthusiastic about responding to the grunts of other bucks. They'll still respond quite readily to a doe grunt, though.

Seasons Past

In the late 1960s I began raking the trails in my hunting areas free of leaves and other debris, which enabled me to reach any stand undetected. It's a tactic that has been much copied, and for good reason, as it's very effective. (Kate Fiduccia)

Here are four dandy bucks that I tracked successfully. Each buck reacted differently to being pursued, and I learned something new on every hunt.

My son, Cody, took his first deer when he was just seven years old. I used a social blat to stop the doe for him. (Kate Fiduccia)

This was Cody's first Texas buck. We drew it from the mesquite cover with a soft guttural grunt, and he dropped the buck in its tracks with one clean shot at 130 yards. (Kate Fiduccia)

I lured this huge Texas buck from cover with an estrus-blat call.

Ralph Somma bagged this terrific buck by calling and rattling it into range. (Ralph Somma)

This big buck was chasing a doe at first light, despite a clear sky and full moon the night before. Although many hunters still insist otherwise, studies have shown that moon phases have no real effect on deer activity or behavior.

My wife, Kate, shows off a Michigan buck she froze with a single trail grunt.

Calling works on virtually all big game animals. I shot this bull in the late 1980s by rattling antlers and making soft cow elk mew sounds, a technique I pioneered. He scored over 350 Boone & Crockett points.

I lured this big bull moose with a cow call while hunting at Tuckamore Lodge in Newfoundland.

Radios should be used for emergencies or important hunting conversation only. Hunters who use radios for continuous, frivolous conversation can count on seeing fewer deer. Motorola now makes a model that vibrates when calls come in and has a voice-activation feature. I strongly recommend using radios with these features.

The prevailing wind appeared to be blowing my scent right toward the area I was watching when I took this muley buck, but my Windicator powder clearly showed the scent was actually being carried up and behind me by a convection current.

Cody with a good management buck shot at Legends Ranch in Michigan. The buck stood still for the shot after the guide blew a tending grunt.

All-terrain vehicles such as this are ideal for carting deer out of the woods. This is my cousin, Leo Somma.

Ralph Somma followed this New York buck's tracks in the snow until he came upon it bedded down with a doe.

Hunters need to understand that does grunt all year, and they're major users of the cohesive grunt, which I think is more accurately termed a social grunt. Does grunt to reprimand fawns, to call in fawns and yearlings, and to warn off young immature bucks. These non-sexual vocalizations can range from a squeal to a deep, guttural sound.

The post rut doe grunt is a prolonged whiney grunt. The doe wants attention and she wants it fast. She roams through the woods making this guttural sound until she gets a response. It sounds something like *Buuurrrrp*. She makes this sound without any continuity. Sometimes she'll make two or three burps in a short period, other times several minutes will pass between calls.

It's an excellent call to imitate, as long as you don't make it loudly.

The post rut buck grunt is an excited sound. The buck is in a rush to find the season's final does in estrus. His intensity is

I took this dandy nine-point buck (note the kicker) after luring him out of some laurels with an enticing doe grunt call. (Kate Fiduccia)

dramatic. This is where many bucks create their undoing, as they ignore everything else in order to get the brass ring. It's a time when all bucks have an equal opportunity to breed. They know it and react accordingly.

Many larger, more aggressive bucks are physically worn to a frazzle by this time. Younger bucks know they now have a better chance of chasing off a buck that was more dominant during the other two phases of the rut.

When grunting during the post rut, you'll have opportunities to see many more bucks than you'd expect. This is the most forgiving period when it comes to grunting. If you're going to get away with making a mistake, it will usually be during this frenzied time frame.

Sometimes, as the saying goes, rules are meant to be broken. Although I'm a major proponent of calling and rattling softly, this is one time when you can call a little more loudly and aggressively and get away with it. Sometimes, to get through to a buck passing by during the post rut, you have to almost double the volume of the soft calls you've been making all season.

The post rut buck grunt is strikingly similar to the primary cadence, except that it's made loudly and repeatedly. It goes this like: *Eeeerp, eeeerp, eeeerp*—pause a few seconds—*eeeerp, eeeerp, eeeerp*—pause a few more seconds—*eeeerp, eeeerp, eeeerp*. When you see a buck, stop calling and let him dictate your next move. If he moves away from you without ever looking your way, call again and stop when he reacts. If you don't see a buck, continue calling every fifteen minutes or so.

Smart Hunting

Ted Rose

Chapter
10

THE RUT

I'll bet dollars to doughnuts that most of you opened the book to this chapter first. That's understandable. What deer hunters typically know about the rut has, for the most part, been hunting lore and techniques passed down by their fathers, grandfathers, and friends. Although some of what they've learned is based on solid knowledge and experience, a lot of this information is mixed with generous portions of old wives' tales and incorrect assumptions.

Today's hunters are fortunate to have a wealth of new information available about deer hunting and the rut in books, on the Internet, and from articles and papers written by biologists and the hunting press. A serious hunter these days knows a deer has thirty-two teeth, knows how to manage a deer herd, understands the importance of selective buck harvesting, can decipher the body language of a deer, and can even name a deer's external glands and how each one functions.

Despite all this knowledge, for a majority of deer hunters the rut remains the most anticipated and least understood part of the hunting season. The first question hunters ask is, "When is the rut?" If I had a dollar for every time a hunter asked me that at seminars or via e-mail, I'd be a very rich man. And I'd be spending that money deer hunting across North America during one of the three distinct periods of the rut.

One of the most persistent fallacies about the breeding season is that the rut is heavily dependent on cold weather. After all, almost everything we heard and read as young hunters emphasized that the best buck hunting happens when cold weather brings in the rut. In fact, during my early hunting years I regularly planned my strategy around cold weather.

I believed in this theory so much that I timed my vacation each year to hunt in the northern regions of New York, where cold weather (in those days) came early and hard and stayed late. Many of these hunts took place in the small town of Childwold, New York, nestled in the foothills of the Adirondack Mountains between Tupper Lake and Cranberry Lake.

This camp is in northern Maine where cold, snowy weather is common during the gun season. A hunt here, or anywhere else in the Northeast, during mid-November is sure to catch some portion of the rut. (Hal Blood)

I often scheduled my vacation in late November, usually around Thanksgiving, when I thought the rut was "on" because of the colder weather. It wasn't until about 1975 that I discovered, through hard experience, a flaw in this philosophy. Over the years, I saw the same amount of breeding activity during that particular week whether it was warm or cold. In addition, as the hunting seasons piled up, it didn't seem to matter whether I was hunting in the southern or northern part of the state. It became evident that cold weather wasn't the single magical element needed to spark the rut.

What I learned during those early years of deer hunting was that cold weather isn't responsible for the onset, or even the intensity, of the whitetail's breeding cycle. Mother Nature, always perfect in her design, just can't rely solely on weather to perpetuate a species. Plain common sense should tell you that.

The role cold weather does actually play is to encourage the diurnal (daytime) activity of deer. It spurs bucks and does to move about much more throughout their territory during the day and in the evening. Bucks are motivated by the crisp temperatures to seek out does, and in extremely cold conditions, extra daytime rutting movement also helps them stay warm.

In a warm rutting period, bucks become lethargic and tend to bed down more throughout the day, taking up the chase at dawn, dusk, and during the cooler nighttime hours. Look at it this way: Are you more motivated to participate in lovemaking during a 95-degree day with high humidity or in the evening when the humidity is gone and the temperature has dropped 20 degrees? So while cold weather doesn't cause the rut, it can certainly push deer to move more throughout the day.

This scenario also holds true for sign like scrapes, licking branches, and rubs left by bucks in the woods and fields. During a warm rut, bucks make fewer scrapes and rubs and leave less

This big bruiser was following a doe at 2:00 in the afternoon on a cold day. Low temperatures simply generate more daytime activity. (Ted Rose)

rut-related sign. They simply aren't motivated to paw out as many scrape sites or rub as many trees. The plain truth is that the warmer temperatures just make them lazier.

As soon as the weather begins to turn colder, however, bucks immediately start leaving rutting sign such as primary scrapes and rubs all over the woods. This obvious overabundance of rut sign is seen by more hunters, who interpret it as an indication that the rut is now in full swing. Hunters become more excited, hunt longer and harder, and therefore see and bag more deer than they do during a warmer rut period when less of this sign is evident.

Unfortunately, when a hunter doesn't see a lot of rubs, scrapes, or bucks chasing does during the day he usually arrives at one of two erroneous conclusions: the rut is late, or, worse yet, it's over. Shockingly, these assumptions lead many hunters to unknowingly hunt the early or late sides of the peak rut. Just remember, warm fall or cold fall, the peak of the rut—and the entire rut—will take place one way or the other. You can take that to the deer hunting bank and deposit it for a future withdrawal.

Nature relies on a much more dependable stimulus mechanism than cold temperatures to set the breeding cycle into motion. Light, or more correctly photoperiodism (except near the equator), is the deciding factor. As fall approaches, the decreasing

This was one of only a few rubs I found on my farm during a warm rut in New York, but just a week later I shot a nice eight-point buck on the trail of a hot doe nearby. Warm weather means less visible signs of rutting activity, but doesn't delay the rut.

ratio of daylight to darkness triggers the start of the mating season. This has even been documented with deer that were moved from one hemisphere to the other. They quickly adjusted their schedule to match the light conditions in their new home.

Recent tests document that the breeding cycle of white-tailed deer is dictated by decreasing light absorbed in a gland in the corner of a buck's eye called the preorbital gland (except in the northernmost and southernmost regions of North America, where there is a significant difference in latitude and the amount of available light). This gland then sends a chemical signal to the brain, which releases hormones throughout the buck's system, which in turn causes his testicles to drop and dramatically raises his testosterone level. The extra chemical raises his "maleness," making him more belligerent to other bucks and less tolerant of their social company. Now he is more inclined to become a loner and to seek out does rather than "hang" with his erstwhile bachelor-group buddies.

From southern Canada to northern Georgia, the whitetail's breeding cycle generally lasts about three months. This means the peak of the primary rut usually takes place from about November 10 through November 25. If you doubt this, search the Web for a deer hunting guide in Saskatchewan, Wisconsin, Maine, or New York. Ask him when you should book a hunt to coincide with the peak of the rut in his area. I'll bet you almost anything that he suggests mid-November.

But as we all know, nothing, not even the rut of the white-tailed deer, is etched in stone. Nature has built in some safety valves that compensate for natural disasters by pushing up, delaying, or even putting off the breeding cycle of deer altogether.

The elements that cause such drastic action are varied. These include stress from a prolonged period of scarce food; a thick layer of ice or very deep snow on the ground over a long period of time; flooding; injury to the doe; periods of extreme cold

My calendar shows the dates and the activity levels of the rut in New York. The last week indicates that the rut is winding down, but it's definitely not over.

or heat over a long time; unusually heavy predation; fire; and even severe overpopulation. Any one of these elements can affect the regular timing of the breeding cycle.

So we know that, aside from catastrophic events like those described above, deer breed regardless of warm or cool temperatures. And we know that the breeding season lasts around three months, with mid-November marking the peak in most areas. But there are also other high and low levels of rutting activity within this three-month period. Many variables come into play. In fact, there is documented evidence of bucks breeding does as early as September and as late as March. While the latter case is rare, it can happen. The bottom line is that whitetails will mate over long periods if the opportunity presents itself.

If a doe hasn't been bred she'll continue coming into estrus every twenty-eight to thirty-two days until she mates successfully.

As long as a buck has antlers on his head, he is ready, willing, and able to breed, albeit less enthusiastically in March than in December, January, or February. He's ready to breed a doe no matter what time of the year it is or how warm it might get. Hunters who understand this and consider it as part of their hunting strategy will put more bucks on the ground.

Let's take a closer look at each of the three distinct stages of the breeding cycle, and at how savvy hunters use them to their advantage.

THE PRE-RUT

The highly productive first rut—often called the preliminary rut, false rut, or pre-rut—is the least capitalized on by hunters. I like to refer to it as the pre-rut because, although not of high intensity, it creates a short burst of activity and draws a lot of bucks and a few mature does to one area.

Generally, this phase of the breeding cycle occurs in mid-October. Just before this period, bucks of the same age-class hang out together in small groups called bachelor herds. Although they can breed soon after they shed their velvet, which occurs as early as the end of August, their primary concern in September and early October is still food.

Bowhunters are usually the first wave of sportsmen and women to take up the hunt for deer each year. As such, they are witness to a lot of deer behavioral changes related to demeanor, food sources, activity levels, and so on. Archers also spot the first rubs and scrapes made by bucks.

Many of you can confirm what I'm about to describe through firsthand experience. Archers, and even early season black-powder enthusiasts, often hunt for several days in an area that doesn't have much sign of rutting activity. You know what I

I found this small pre-rut scrape in October, although it wasn't worth hunting over. When you notice a sudden and dramatic increase in the number of scrapes and rubs in a specific area, the hunting will be much better.

mean. You might notice an occasional rub and perhaps a small scrape that looks old and dried up, but not much else.

Then the very next day, quite unexpectedly, you find several fresh scrapes that weren't there just twenty-four hours earlier. And they look like active scrapes. They're usually small in size, pawed to bare ground, and may even be muddy and have a strong musky odor. You have just observed a yearly phenomenon related to the rut. So what happens to cause this obvious intense breeding activity in bucks? Nature has just initiated the pre-rut, also known, sadly for the bucks, as the false rut.

Here is the scenario. As a bachelor group of bucks departs from bedding areas to feed, they aren't thinking of anything but gathering food. They casually stroll through the woods, sometimes in groups of two or more, eating acorns or leaves full of sugar or perhaps heading to an apple orchard. Then out of nowhere they're met by the estrus pheromones of a mature estrus doe. *Wham!* It's like a cold slap in the face, and a flurry of intense activity begins. Bucks that scent the estrus odor immediately forget about food and begin to make small but numerous scrapes, hoping to attract the hot doe. They also make rubs for the same reason. They are all incredibly excited. You would be too if you had to wait a year for you-know-what!

I believe they're also somewhat confused. Their immediate instinctive reaction includes running all over the woods seeking out potential hot does. Mother Nature uses the pre-rut to intentionally knock the buck over the head, so to speak, to alert him to the onset of the breeding season. From this point on, bucks think more about mating and less about food.

This early estrus cycle is confined to only the most mature of does in any given herd (4½ to 5½ years old). This group performs a vital service by coming into their cycle first: getting the rut started. Contrary to popular belief, it isn't males who initiate the rut. Not by a long shot. The mature doe population determines the onset of the rut and, to some degree, its intensity. It's just like a mature woman in her prime; her menstrual cycle is predictable and reliable. With younger women, however, their period may be less dependable and they may even skip a cycle here and there— especially during stressful times.

The estrus cycle of young does is less reliable, as is the cycle of does past their prime. Think about what occurs in female dogs. Young female dogs experience erratic estrus cycles, while mature bitches in their prime come into a reliable estrus cycle twice a year. But as the female dog grows old, her cycle becomes erratic again and inevitably it stops completely.

Unfortunately for the bucks, this false rut lasts only twenty-four to thirty-six hours, typically somewhere around October 15 to 20 each year. Then it's finished, leaving bucks frustrated, angry, and confused — just like Mother Nature wants them to be.

Only a few lucky bucks that quickly locate these hot mature does get to service them. The rest are left out in the cold.

This false rut is instrumental in quickly breaking up the bachelor herds. Bucks are no longer tolerant of each other, becoming more belligerent day by day. As October winds down, they often engage in immediate aggressive behavior and spar willingly with other bucks. The building tension and continuing decrease in daylight also caused them to take out their frustration on the nearest sapling or tree. This is nature's way of helping to deposit the scent from their foreheads in order to leave a chemical message to other competing bucks and possible receptive does. This activity also helps strengthen their neck muscles, getting them physically and mentally prepared for the more serious battles that are sure to come over the next several weeks.

The pre-rut sometimes begins as early as October 10. So the next time you're hunting and notice that there is no scrape sign one day, and then fresh scrape activity almost everywhere in the woods the next day, write down the date. Now count twenty-eight to thirty-two days forward, which reveals when the second stage of the rut, called the primary rut, will kick in. As I'll relate in the pages below, this is the most active breeding phase.

Hunters can employ a variety of strategies to bag a nice buck during the false rut in October. Non-aggressive rattling and making soft estrus doe blats are two excellent techniques at this time of year. Just remember not to be overly aggressive. Bucks are getting excited, but they aren't fired up enough to respond strongly yet. Creating mock scrapes, rub grunting, and gently shaking brush and saplings will all dramatically increase your odds of success during this first period of the rut.

Subdued rattling for bucks during these two to three days usually brings an immediate response from bucks frustrated by not finding a willing doe to breed. When they hear a soft clicking of antlers, they think they've discovered a buck protecting his hot doe from another buck. Their strategy is to try to sneak in and out with the doe long before the other two bucks notice. Just keep your rattling sequence toned down.

By the way, mature does undergoing the early, brief estrus cycle are also eager to respond to this hunting technique. And there is no better lure than rattling in a hot doe, because a horny buck is sure to follow.

I keep detailed records of my encounters with bucks during the false rut. These records show how productive this early rut

Bucks often mistake the sounds of a portable tree stand going up (scraping bark and small twigs snapping) with noises other bucks make while rubbing trees or fighting.

can be. I remember making an entry about rattling in several good bucks one day during the false rut in New York State. The entry was made on October 10.

I was slowly putting up my portable tree stand. Now and then it hit small branches, snapping them off the tree trunk. After a few minutes I heard a deer crash down the mountainside toward me. (I later realized that the cracking branches must have sounded like two bucks in a shoving match.) I stopped climbing mid-tree and waited to see what would happen.

Within moments, I spotted a large-racked buck trotting toward me. I could hear him grunting very softly as he got within fifteen yards. His eyes were bulging from his head. He noticed me seconds later. To my surprise, the buck totally ignored me and paced defiantly around the tree several times. He then walked off a few yards, pawed up a small scrape, and left, grunting continually all the while. Unfortunately, I didn't have a chance to get to my bow, which was still at the base of the tree stand.

The buck probably thought there were two other bucks fighting over one of the few does in estrus at the time. Throwing caution to the wind, he came in ready and willing to meet the challenge head-on. When he left, I thought my best opportunity had disappeared as well. Once I got set up, though, I rattled the determined buck back in only thirty minutes later. But this time he never came close enough for a shot. Over the next few hours, I rattled in three more bucks.

Another demonstration of the success a hunter can have during the pre-rut happened on October 13, 1989. It was 1 PM, and I had just finished my first grunting sequence when I heard a twig snap. I watched a really big buck recklessly walk through a patch of second-growth timber just out of range from my tree stand. Grunting and drooling from the corner of his mouth, he walked around the area several times before departing.

I waited a few minutes and tried grunting him back. When he didn't respond, I became a bit depressed. As I sat there feeling sorry for myself, I heard the soft grunting of a deer behind me. A small six-point emerged directly under my stand and paced around nervously for several minutes before leaving. I waited a little while and then grunted. Within a few minutes yet another buck responded, an eight-pointer this time. As I drew on the buck, he looked at me, turned inside out, and bolted away as my arrow sailed harmlessly over his back.

I blew one more grunt, not thinking for a moment that I would attract still another buck after all the activity I'd already seen. I did. This time, however, things were slightly different. After grunting softly for several minutes, a doe stepped out, looked around, urinated, and walked off. Another eight-pointer appeared moments behind her, and with a purposeful walk he slowly followed her trail. He never saw me stand, draw, and release the arrow because all his attention was focused on the hot doe's scent. As the buck ran off a short way before surrendering to his fatal injury, two more bucks walked past my stand.

Needless to say, the false rut can generate unimaginable success for hunters who know when to expect it and how to take advantage of it. The next time you're hunting in October and you discover a host of scrapes that seem to magically appear overnight, set up in a good spot during the next twenty-four to thirty-six hours and expect to see some fast action.

THE PRIMARY RUT

As I mentioned earlier, if you count twenty-eight days or so forward from the pre-rut, you'll be right in the peak time of the primary rut. Most of the does in any herd come into estrus during this middle phase of the three ruts. Peak activity lasts for about two weeks or so.

I marked the peak of the pre-rut as October 31, so I knew the peak of the primary rut would come twenty-eight to thirty-two days later. This knowledge allowed me to take the buck shown here as he followed a doe.

In the latitudes from roughly Saskatchewan, Wisconsin, Maine, and New York down through the Midwest and Mid-Atlantic regions to around northern Georgia, the primary rut occurs from November 10 through 15, give or take a few days on either side. Any mature does that came into estrus twenty-eight days earlier but weren't bred come into estrus again during this period.

I've talked about this several times with Justin B. Henry, owner of a hunting lodge in Sherwood Park, Alberta. Henry is famous for having guided clients to some of the largest, most heavily racked whitetail bucks in North America. During one conversation, I asked Henry when he thought I should hunt at his lodge.

"I'd be a fool if I had you here any other time than the peak of the primary rut," he said. "A good time would be during the second or third week of November." Now Henry's lodge is in Canada, where it's cold and snowy early in the season, yet the peak of the primary rut occurs at the same time as it does in the eastern U.S.

If you still need convincing that this is a wide and reliable phenomenon across much of the continent, here's the testimony of Gene Wensel, a peer and friend who lives out West. He says that in his home state of Montana, "Our doe deer normally come into heat about November 16 through 18 on an annual basis. This peak lasts for a week or so at a fever pitch." That's Montana, folks. And the dates are very close to the same dates I suggest as the peak of the rut throughout New England and the rest of the country.

The peak time of aggressive activity occurs roughly a week to ten days before the primary rut. Bucks are *really* frustrated, and

I shot this Montana buck in mid-November in the late 1980s. He was hot on the heels of an estrus doe, like bucks throughout most of whitetail country at this time of year.

they're now doing more than just jousting for position as they did in the pre-rut. They're looking for trouble and are deadly serious about any encounter they have with another buck, especially transient bucks they don't know at all. These encounters can range from quick fights to down-and-out life-ending contests because the bucks are playing for all the marbles now. If you rattle for deer, now is the time you can rattle more aggressively and still have success.

If you're a rattler, you can now put a little more feeling into it. However, I'll repeat here again that I don't believe in overly aggressive hunting tactics. Despite what you might have read or heard from other experts, I can assure you that even when bucks are at their most aggressive, they fail to respond to seriously aggressive tactics. No buck, regardless of his size or level of sexual frustration, wants to have a physical encounter with another buck that may wind up seriously injuring him.

Think back to your high school days. Did you ever know anyone who picked a fight with someone who was obviously taller, stronger, and heavier? I'll bet the answer is a resounding no. Even if you were one of the toughest guys in school, odds are that when you had a fight it was with someone who was of similar or lesser size.

Deer are no different. Within the male whitetail's society, the pecking order is established mostly by body language during the spring and summer months when the bucks are in velvet. By the time a buck sheds his velvet, he is well aware of his rank in the herd. He knows who his superiors are, as well as his equals and his subordinates. He only tests his status with equals or subordinates, should they be so daring, during the mating season.

You will be a lonely hunter if you adopt harshly aggressive calling or rattling tactics. Trust me, this will usually push bucks far away from your location.

Making your calls or your rattles sound submissive draws the attention of bucks of all sizes, especially big, so-called dominant bucks. These mature bucks realize that most of the time all they have to do to scare off a submissive buck is exhibit aggressive body language. The exception occurs when a physically stronger buck with a rack of equal or slightly smaller size decides to fight with a buck that has a bigger body and rack.

The smaller buck may have reserve energy because he hasn't undergone as much stress as the larger buck. He may not have even had as many fights. Therefore, he is much fresher than the worn-out bigger buck. He may temporarily overpower the larger buck, take his position in the hierarchy, and become the leader of the herd until he too is ejected from power.

THE POST RUT

Let's get back to the rut. Count twenty-eight forward from the primary rut date and you arrive at the peak time for the late rut, which is the third phase of the white-tailed deer's breeding cycle.

During the late rut, most of the year's fawns and yearling does—and any other doe that wasn't successfully bred or that skipped a cycle during the last period—come into a potent estrus cycle and are bred. It is nature's way of ensuring the perpetuation of the species.

Many hunters have great success with tactics like decoying, rattling, and calling in this phase. This doesn't surprise me, as rattling and calling can be effective well into January and February. That's because some does in the heart of the country are still experiencing estrus cycles in December. In southern parts of the country, many does come into heat in late January or on through February.

The adaptable, innovative hunter understands that the rut can last a quarter of the year. More importantly, he uses this information to plan a lethal whitetail strategy. Some strategies include patterning bucks, although bucks are harder to pattern

I like to use decoys early in the bow season and again during the late rut, when they're most effective. Note this buck's body language as he approaches the decoy. (Ted Rose)

during the post rut in heavily hunted areas in the Northeast because they must substantially extend their territory in order to locate late-season estrus does.

The tactics that pay big dividends during this period usually involve imitating bucks seeking out does in estrus. Once a buck thinks he can hear, smell, or see another buck chasing a doe in estrus, he is sure to investigate in hopes of getting the doe himself.

Other late-rut strategies include rattling, calling, mock scrapes, using decoys (both male and female), laying mock urine trails, and using new techniques such as Shake, Rattle, & Roll (shaking saplings, rattling antlers, and rolling brush and leaves). In addition, some traditional tactics can bring success. These methods include posting near well-traveled runways along secluded swamps and ridges, watching and waiting along the edges of agricultural fields, and ambushing deer in social areas.

During the third phase of the rut, a single doe in estrus can attract several bucks. Not all at once, of course, but over several hours many bucks may pick up and follow the trail. The patient hunter often comes home with a trophy during this exciting stage. I regularly pass up lesser bucks that obviously have been on the trail of one of these hot does, eventually bagging a bigger buck as a result.

One such incident occurred while I was hunting on the ridge behind my home. It was December 19, and I was hunting the black-powder season that starts the day after the regular firearm season ends. Two days earlier I had noticed a flurry of rut activity after not seeing a buck in this area for several days previous. Knowing that the post rut was due, I immediately realized the activity I saw was from the bucks that had scented the pheromones left by an estrus doe or two. (Keep in mind that the post rut is similar to the pre-rut in that it is relatively short in comparison to the primary rut.)

I decided to hunt the area for the next two days from a tree stand that overlooked a social area. On the last day of the season, I watched four different bucks walk up the trail without ever lifting their noses from the ground. The first two bucks were small four- and six-pointers. The third buck was a decent eight-pointer. I was contemplating shooting him when I spotted an even better buck making his way up the same trail about one hundred yards away. As he trotted slowly past my stand with his nose glued to the ground, I ended his pursuit of this estrus doe with one clean shot.

You don't have to be a rocket scientist to identify and capitalize on methods for taking good bucks during the late rut. Except in the South, snow usually covers the ground at this time of year. This presents an ideal opportunity for hunters to narrow down their search of a doe in estrus. Obviously, if you can locate a hot doe, it won't be long before you also locate bucks trailing her.

Hunters often spot pink or red droppings left by an estrus doe as she urinates in the snow. Because there aren't many does in heat during the post rut, interested bucks may come in from great distances. This is also a great time to pick up the track of a good buck doing some tracking of his own. His mind is so focused on the doe ahead of him that he often forgets to watch his back trail. I have one thing to say to a buck who offers me that opportunity: "Trail your doe, my pretty. Trail your doe."

Once I've located hot doe sign, I try to figure out the route she is traveling. Keep in mind, as with bucks, does are difficult to pattern, especially in heavily hunted areas. They too have increased their overall range in search of mates. The difference now is that there are far more bucks ready to service an estrus doe than there were during the primary rut, when an estrus doe had a substantial amount of competition from other does.

During the post rut an estrus doe has only to follow her normal routes and amorous bucks will enthusiastically seek her out. By keeping track of her travels, you will inevitably find yourself at the right place at the right time to take a buck.

Although the false and primary ruts get a lot of attention from hunters, the post rut continues to be the red-headed stepchild. Hunters mostly ignore this phase because they mistakenly believe that the rut is long over, or perhaps they're tired of hunting by the end of the rutting season and don't effectively interpret rutting behavior and sign.

Next season, keep your chin up if you're still looking to score on a buck when the post rut arrives. The best may be yet to come.

PHASE FOUR

This is a phase of the rut that many hunters don't recognize. It occurs under certain extenuating circumstances that typically relate to extreme weather patterns during the normal phases of the primary and post-rut stages of the breeding cycle. Only a few does experience this late, late phase of estrus during the months of January and February, but the few that do quickly attract bucks. Biologists are beginning to better understand this breeding phenomenon, and there should be some interesting and exciting documentation over the next few years regarding this "extra" phase of the rut.

THE FRENZY PERIOD

Now that we've examined the phases of the rut, here is some additional information you probably haven't heard before. It will help you maximize your chances during the chaotic days of the rut.

Most hunters assume that the best time to take a buck is during the peak phase of the primary rut, and to a large degree this is true, but it can also be misleading. While it is certainly a fact that bucks are looking for does during the peak of the primary rut, bucks that rank high in status are most likely already hooked up with a doe in estrus. These bucks are the ones so often heard about that mindlessly follow a doe in estrus through the woods and inevitably get intercepted and shot by hunters.

Although the peak of the rut certainly presents these types of opportunities, if you really want to be successful while hunting the primary phase of the rut you should be ready to hunt several days *before* you think the actual peak of the breeding will take place.

By hunting just a few days prior to the peak, you increase your chances of seeing more bucks and taking a big bruiser ten times over. I call this the "frenzy period" of the primary rut. This phase has an obvious frenetic appearance to it because most of the does begin to come into estrus and emit that magic odor. The other, shorter breeding periods just don't include this overwhelming number of estrus does.

Although does are discharging an estrus pheromone, they are not ready to breed yet. Basically, this foreplay by the does is designed to excite as many bucks as possible. As more does come into heat, the pheromone begins to dominate the whitetail buck's world. As discussed earlier, the bucks become extremely aggressive toward each other and will no longer tolerate the presence of other males.

While the pheromone puts the buck in an excited sexual state, he remains frustrated until the estrus cycle reaches the point where a doe actually accepts his advances to mount and breed her. Actual copulation is quick and often happens over a period of twenty-four to forty-eight hours.

But before this acceptance takes place, bucks are so excited by the estrus pheromone that they will, at times, masturbate due to their frustration at not being able to breed yet (much like bull elk do). As the odor of the pheromone gets stronger and stronger, bucks literally go haywire. They chase every single doe they see to check her current estrus status. If they can't visually locate a doe, they run pell-mell through the woods and fields and up and down mountainsides searching out does that are leaving these tantalizing scents scattered throughout their range.

My Stat Card records over the last thirty years show that the frenzy period fell between November 10 and 13 the majority of the time. Some years, it occurred from November 7 to 10, and other years from November 12 to 15.

Generally, the frenzy period lasts forty-eight to ninety-six hours, although in warm seasons it may run on the low side. It is unmistakable. If you're driving to work after November 1 and you happen to see a big-racked buck zigzagging through an open field, call in sick. The frenzy period is on! Other indicators include bucks running along fence lines in the middle of the day, bucks darting from wood lines into fields and back, and any other abnormal buck activity, especially around midday.

If you notice a buck acting particularly defiant, you can bet the frenzy is on. Let me explain what I mean by defiant bucks. While calling or rattling I've often encountered bucks that, for one reason or another, "make" me. Most times, these bucks turn themselves inside out and hightail it back into cover. (There are exceptions, of course, but this is by and large true.) However, as the primary rut gets closer and the estrus pheromones become more widespread, the general attitude of a buck changes.

I immediately know the frenzy period has begun when bucks exhibit very unusual, even belligerent behavior when faced with my presence. Many of these bucks have stared me down, as if to say, "Yeah, what do you want?" Others, after clearly identifying me as a human from only a few yards away, continued to casually walk past me almost as if I didn't exist. Obviously, a buck showing this type of behavior smells something so powerful that he ignores the danger nearby.

Still other times, I've seen bucks with their eyes bugged out come zigzagging past my stand, disappearing into the brush as quickly as they appeared. They reappear moments later and repeat the process again and again, sometimes for many minutes. This kind of behavior is a definite indication that these bucks have forsaken their normal fear of humans and are preoccupied with only one thought: sex. Their behavior is understandable.

Hunting this frenzy period will be like no other type of hunting you've ever experienced. No matter where you live, every primary rut phase is preceded by this two- to four-day stage. I regularly recommend that hunters plan their vacations around this period. These are often the best few days of hunting in the entire season. It certainly beats hunting during the opening week of the firearm season.

You can take advantage of this frenzy period everywhere in whitetail country by doing a little investigating as to the specific times in your area and then fine-tuning your approach over a year or two.

One of the best ways to determine if the frenzy period has begun is to start reading the vehicle accident report section of your local newspaper a few days before Halloween. If you live in the city, have someone from your hunting area start mailing you a local paper. Each week you'll see a definite increase in the number of car/deer accidents reported. You can bet it's because careless bucks are seeking out does emitting more estrus pheromones.

There will always be some level of controversy among hunters about the rut and when it occurs throughout North America. Don't let that dissuade you from confidently believing in and applying what you've just read. I guarantee that it will lead to more shot opportunities.

TIMING THE RUT

PRE-RUT

Generally begins about October 13 and includes a high activity level for one to two days, extending an additional day or so depending on variable factors. Then it abruptly ends.

PRIMARY RUT

Starts with the frenzy period around November 10 to 15, give or take a few days. It continues into the period where bucks and does are matched up for a week and then there's a slight decline in breeding activity around November 22 or 23.

Continued on next page

LATE RUT

Around December 13 sexual activity rises again, with bucks going into an excited state for two or three days that then declines steadily until roughly December 25. Generally, if a hunter counts twenty-eight days between peaks of sexual activity, he will discover the heart of the frenzy period during each of the three phases.

Chapter
11

READING THE WIND

Over the years I've regularly espoused a single tactic over all others when it comes to hunting bucks, especially mature whitetail bucks: "Bust a buck's nose and you've busted the buck."

Yes, I know, we've all been bored to death by the endless articles on how effective a deer's nose is and how important it is to keep your clothes and body clean and to always keep the wind in your face. Well, I'm about to bore you one more time, because if you want to consistently take big bucks keeping your scent out of their nostrils is paramount.

There are two factors in not allowing scent to betray you: know how to hunt all the different aspects of wind and know how to reduce the unnatural odors that alarm a deer.

Start by paying attention to the direction of the wind, which is nothing more than a collection of air currents. Knowing and understanding these currents, thermals, convections, and prevailing breezes is key to understanding the factors of wind.

White-tailed deer, especially bucks, predominantly survive through their sense of smell. A buck may question what he sees, and he may doubt a message from his ears, but he never under any circumstances doubts the messages his nose sends to his brain. Deer constantly utilize wind direction to aid their movement, particularly when determining the relative safety of the paths they're traveling. Therefore, we must be as knowledgeable about wind as possible in order to be the best hunters, or predators, we can be.

There are several components associated with wind. Meteorologists define wind as air in horizontal motion relative to the surface of the earth. This atmospheric motion is better identified

To fool bucks consistently, you must learn to read all types of air currents. (Ted Rose)

as ascending or descending currents, and not wind at all. As a hunter, you should always decipher from which direction the wind is coming because this tells you whether the wind will be cooler, warmer, drier, or more humid than the air you're in. Also note the makeup of the wind. Is it beginning to shift or is it holding steady from a certain direction? A change of wind direction could very well be a sign that a high pressure system is about to move into your area. If you're able to pick up this sign, you can use the information to better plan your hunting strategy.

The wind normally picks up during the day with the increase in the air temperature, and it slows down in the late afternoon. This accounts for why so many of us have witnessed a heavy wind dying down just before dusk. If the wind doesn't slow down come sunset, the barometric pressure is going to change. And deer movement increases with changes in barometric pressure. If there is very little change in the wind speed throughout the day, then the current weather conditions aren't likely to change. In this case, deer won't move more than normal and you may want to try more active hunting tactics.

PREVAILING WIND

Every area you hunt will have a prevailing wind direction. Seasoned hunters learn to pay meticulous attention to prevailing winds. Throughout much of the U.S., wind typically emanates from the north or northwest. This prevailing wind direction is crucial to hunters who are considering where to position a stand, especially when posting in a field, natural bottleneck, or ravine.

If you ignore the prevailing wind direction, your scent could be picked up by a deer approaching your stand. The deer will slip away unnoticed long before you have an opportunity to spot it. You may spend hours on a stand without seeing a single deer simply because your scent was spread by a current of air you didn't take into account.

Prevailing winds are easy to determine in virtually any area, and barring some unusual circumstance, a hunter can count on these air currents blowing in the same direction day in and day out.

CONVECTION CURRENTS

Convection currents differ from prevailing winds in that they're specific to a particular section of terrain. They seem to have a mind of their own, often blowing in an entirely different direction, or directions, than the prevailing breeze. These wind currents can wreak havoc on your deer hunting if you don't understand how they work.

I first learned about convection currents twenty-five years ago. I knew the direction the prevailing breeze came from a majority of the time within a certain area that I hunted. So I set up on a ridgetop overlooking a steep draw, figuring my scent would be carried away from approaching deer.

After sitting in my stand for about an hour or so, I heard the distinct crunching of leaves as deer moved into the area. "Excellent," I thought, "the wind is blowing perfectly. They'll never know I'm here." Moments later, I saw two small bucks approach my stand. Unconcerned, they steadily moved down the trail. About fifty yards out, both bucks jammed on the brakes and skidded along the carpet of fallen leaves. Without an instant's hesitation, they whirled around and disappeared back from where they came.

I was dumbfounded, and soon began working through all the reasons they might have spooked. I hadn't walked anywhere in the area from which they approached, and unless another hunter had, I just couldn't understand what went wrong. The wind gently and steadily blew against my face, so it never oc-curred to me that air currents could be the culprit.

That evening I told a friend about what happened. This fel-low was a high school science teacher, and although he didn't hunt, he had an immediate explanation for what might have hap-pened to spook the deer.

"You understand," he said, "that even though you positioned yourself with the prevailing wind in your favor, the breeze could have been upset or changed as it continued down toward you by some specific feature or features of the terrain at the exact loca-tion of your stand don't you?"

"Uh, no," I replied.

He explained what a convection current was and how it could move directly opposite a prevailing current.

Basically, this air current develops where the prevailing wind meets a change in the landscape—a large boulder; an upsurge in land; a rock wall; a tightly knit group of mature evergreens; a ridge, saddle, valley, or bowl; or any other solid object with enough mass to deflect air. These objects cause the prevailing wind to swirl around them in different directions before sending what's left of the air cur-rent on its way. Convection currents often move in a vertical plane, sending your scent up and down and even in large loops. Mean-while, the prevailing wind could be blowing steadily into your face.

So I had been sitting on my stand with the prevailing wind blowing toward me, completely unaware that the large rock ledge behind me was forcing the wind to loop back toward the two on-coming bucks.

I never forgot that lesson. Whenever I set up to post in an area these days, I hang a large strand of black sewing thread from a branch or from my gun or bow so I can watch how it blows in contrast to the prevailing wind direction. In addition, I use a powder wind detector. Every half hour or so, I squirt blaze-orange

Obstacles like this ledge can push convection currents in virtually any direction, even directly opposite the prevailing breeze.

talcum powder (available from a variety of hunting manufacturers) into the air to pick up any nuances in wind direction.

The string sometimes suggests a slight change in direction, but the powder always shows exactly how chaotic the convection current really is. I am often amazed as I watch the powder rise slowly into the breeze. Often the powder is forced forward or to the side and is swiftly carried off in a direction other than the prevailing wind.

While most times I see the powder travel to my left or right, at other times it quickly falls to the ground and moves out in front of me thirty or forty yards, only to be picked up by the prevailing wind again and carried back in my direction. This phenomenon is one that most deer hunters, even seasoned veterans, never believe until they witness it. I wonder how many hunters have sat on stand all day without seeing an animal and then grumbled about hunting pressure, the stand position, or other factors when their own scent was really to blame.

Even after I understood how complicated a convection current could be, a tricky one still put me on the losing end of an evening's hunt. I had been playing the shell game with my tree stand in one of my favorite areas because of a change in the prevailing wind. That afternoon I moved the stand closer to a group of large pine trees. I set the stand up and was happy that several large overhanging branches above me offered cover, helped hide any movement, and broke up my outline. The wind was blowing directly from where I expected the deer to be moving. Everything seemed perfect; even the cross breeze was in my favor.

Around 4:20 PM a doe stepped out of the brush and cautiously made her way toward me. She stopped every few steps to smell the air. On her heels was a racked buck. I never had a chance to count how many points he had or assess his size. I didn't even have time to draw my bow before the doe let out a screeching alarm-distress snort. Both the buck and doe crashed off into the woods and ran down the ledge to the fields below. I was positive they had heard another hunter or picked up his scent, because only a half hour before they appeared I had checked the wind for any annoying convection currents. Everything had been in my favor.

Soon after they left I sprayed powder into the air again. I was shocked at what I saw. Instead of slowly drifting up and away behind me as it had done earlier, the powder now hung up momentarily in the heavy pine branches just a foot or two above my head and then swiftly fell to the ground and moved out to my left at an angle, right to the spot where the doe blew the alarm-distress snort.

Upon reflection, I realized there had been a change in the humidity, which could have affected the convection current's direction despite the short time frame. So don't be bashful about using powder to check how the convection currents are moving while in your stand. These tricky currents can change in an instant.

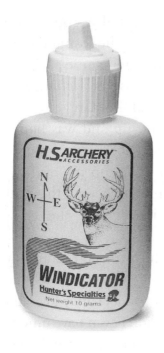

Powder reveals the subtle differences in wind direction that can take place just yards from your stand. (H.S. Scents)

A good way to keep track of air currents is to make entries in a log book. After sitting in a certain stand for several days, take note of the convection currents and how they differ from the direction of the prevailing wind. Jot them down and refer to them before future hunts.

Air that is cooling off can also cause a convection current, although this is less common than the reasons described above.

THERMAL CURRENT

Another air current that hunters should understand is called a thermal current. This current has specific characteristics, and it's most active in early morning and late evening, when hunters are typically in the woods.

At dawn, when temperatures usually begin to rise, the thermal current direction, or flow, is upward. As evening approaches, air temperatures begin to cool off and thermal currents begin to fall. So a hunter who takes a stand at dawn should position himself above the area where he expects to see deer. His scent will rise away from the deer. However, the same stand should be avoided in the evening because the hunter's scent will be carried downhill, provided that there are no physical obstacles in the terrain to cause a devious convection current.

You can overcome thermal current problems by acting the same way a buck would. All bucks have alternate runways leading to and from bedding areas. A buck that has survived even a couple of seasons has learned how to keep the prevailing winds blowing in his face. Some bucks also prefer to keep the wind coming toward them from the right or left. Other bucks are sneaky enough to travel with the wind directly at their backs so they can scent danger coming from behind. They rely on their eyes and ears to pick up danger up ahead.

A seasoned hunter learns to always keep wind uppermost in his mind. And he has alternate stands in his hunting area and uses them to take the best possible advantage of conflicting thermal, convection, or prevailing wind currents.

We all smell, and there isn't a hunter in the world who can escape this fact. No matter how meticulously you try to control scent, it's impossible to eliminate it completely. Once a whitetail enters a specific range close to the hunter absolutely nothing prevents it from picking up human scent, even those expensive carbon hunting suits. The knowledgeable hunter understands this and tries to minimize human odor as much as possible while still playing the wind during every hunt.

So keep your scent to a minimum and pay attention to the direction of prevailing winds, thermals, and convection currents to dramatically increase your chances of seeing and bagging cagey bucks.

Ted Rose

Chapter
12

MOON PHASE—
FACT OR FICTION

Over the last ten years I've been asked some version of the following question over and over: What role does the moon play in deer activity and the rut?

Many deerstalkers are convinced that whitetail activity, especially rutting behavior, is highest during specific moon phases. Some hunters feel the moon's cycle is such an important factor in deer movement that they don't bother to hunt if it isn't at the right stage. Well, I agree that the gravitational pull of the moon is strong and that it does affect some things in our world. For instance, there is no denying the moon's influence on ocean tides. But can we really make the leap from this fact to planning our entire deer season around phases of the moon? I'd like to put this issue to rest once and for all.

I often talk with hunters who claim they see more deer moving during the midday hours after particularly dark nights as a result of the cycle of a new moon. The assumption is that dark nights make it difficult for deer to move easily within their range, forcing them to compensate by moving more during daylight hours. Still others are certain the primary rut takes place during the "rutting moon," which is close to the second full moon after the autumnal equinox.

So-called "hunting experts" have been linking lunar phases to deer activity for decades, but believe me, there are a lot of facts to suggest otherwise. Researchers from the University of Georgia's School of Forest Resources have examined the moon's lunar phases and how each affects the timing of whitetail breeding behavior. They wanted to find out if deer hunters looking to bag a buck were better off concentrating their hunting efforts during a full, new, or partial moon. They also attempted to find out if any of the moon's cycles actually make a difference at all.

UGA wildlife research biologists David Osborn, Dr. Karl Miller, and Robert Warren started by using breeding date information from a variety of state wildlife agencies to determine whether moon phases had any effect on whitetail doe estrus cycles and, therefore, the rutting activities and behavior of bucks. Breeding dates for captive deer were gathered in four states and for more than two thousand free-ranging does in seven others. Believe it or not, this information took from three to nineteen years to compile. It was then compared to lunar cycles.

"We would expect annual breeding dates for a population to be similar if the calendar date—and therefore the same length of daylight—was the driving influence," explained Osborn. "We would expect annual breeding to be less similar if moon phase is the driving influence because a particular moon phase might vary as much as twenty-eight days across years."

But the fact is, biologists and scientists have long agreed that photoperiod (the length of daylight) is the overriding influence on whitetail breeding activity. The phase of the moon has virtually nothing to do with it.

For years, state wildlife biologists all over North America regularly and confidently use calendar dates to help deer hunters plan their time afield to match as closely with peak rut activities as possible. The state of Virginia, for instance, shows November 15 as the peak of the rut, while Minnesota hunters are advised to be in their deer stands the first week of November. As I've

My son, Cody, poses next to an eight-point buck I tracked and shot on the morning after a night with a full moon.

mentioned elsewhere in this book, I generally list the prime rutting dates in most northern states and provinces as roughly November 10 through 15.

While any of these dates can be used as a reliable guideline, they should not be taken as the last word on rutting activity. There are simply too many other factors to consider. For example, if aspects of its environment are putting stress on a doe, Mother Nature steps in to prevent her from coming into heat. This, in turn, prevents the doe from becoming pregnant, avoiding altogether the possibility of losing her fetus or even her own life when times are tough. Instead, the doe skips a cycle or two and waits to come into heat after the stressful conditions have passed.

It usually takes a severe change in conditions to affect the rut. If there is a very early and deep snowfall, unseasonably warm or frigid weather, a lack of nutritious vegetation, or even an absence of mature breeding bucks within the range, a doe may become stressed enough to skip a heat cycle. Absent such extremes, the rut usually takes place right on time across North America.

In the University of Georgia study, Dr. Warren noted that weather, food availability, human activity, and a variety of other factors all play a role in the timing of the rut, but breeding activity typically happens within a relatively predictable period no matter what the moon phase happens to be. Again, length of daylight is the primary element controlling the rut.

The bottom line is that evolution has developed a plan where fawn survival rates are maximized. If fawns are born too early in the year, when it may still be too cold or wet, the does may not be able to gather enough food for themselves to provide vital nutrition in their milk. If they are born too late, fawns may encounter early snowfalls that don't allow them time to become healthy enough to survive the oncoming winter.

If the moon-phase theory were correct, it would mean that fawns could be born twenty-eight days before or after the peak fawn birth date. Yet birthing takes place pretty much the same time every year.

It is important to note that while the rut may occur around the same dates in places like Montana and Maine, breeding activity in the northernmost latitudes of Saskatchewan and Alberta typically takes place over a short period of time. But this activity tends to be a lot more intense.

On the other side of the coin, deer that live down in south Texas and Florida have a much longer breeding season, sometimes lasting four months or more. This means that trying to pin down an actual date for peak rut may be much more difficult in southern areas because rut activity isn't as focused.

Either way, the general consensus among whitetail experts—and almost all of the biologists and scientists I've talked with—is that no matter where deer live they don't seem to pay attention to the phase of the moon.

This ten-point bruiser was taken during a moon cycle that supposedly discourages buck activity. My advice is to ignore the moon phases and hunt as much as you can.

Now that we've debunked the rumor that the moon specifically affects rut timing, let's address whether it plays any role in other aspects of deer life. Do deer really feed more during the day in a new moon phase because they can't gather enough forage on particularly dark nights? Do the moon's cycles have any effect on deer movement in general? Well, according to my deer observations over the last forty years, the answer to both those questions is a resounding "No." And no biologist I've ever talked to or interviewed has found any distinct or predictable patterns in wildlife activity during various phases of the moon.

General deer movement would probably remain fairly consistent if weather, hunting pressure, and food sources remained constant, but the chances of that are slim because deer live in a world of constant change.

Biologists usually agree that the availability of high-quality forage is the most influential factor in deer breeding patterns and movements. Nature makes sure that the driving force behind the life of every doe is procreation, and does respond to changing food sources throughout the year in order to provide the maximum amount of energy for their fetuses or fawns.

Both private and public studies have demonstrated that breeding activity can take place very early or very late, depending on the quality of the mast crop. When the mast crop is heavy and early, does come into heat earlier than normal. If there is a total mast crop failure, then breeding activity might be delayed up to a month or more.

I strongly recommend that hunters quit worrying about what role the moon's cycle plays in their deer hunting, and instead try to keep abreast of conditions in their hunting territory throughout the year. Always look for any extremes in weather, forage, and so on, but base your hunting on the calendar, not the moon.

I start hunting as soon as the season opens, and like many of you I hunt right through to the end. A day in the woods always beats one at home. So use the above information to get the most out of your time afield, but don't let anything deter you from getting out as much as possible, particularly when you see incautious bucks out and about in the midday hours.

Chapter
13

UNORTHODOX DECOY TACTICS

If there is one thing I've learned during my years of deer hunting it's that to be a better deer hunter, you have to be a great pretender. Most of us heard about or saw the movie *Catch Me If You Can* with Leonardo DiCaprio, in which he acts out Frank Abagnale's true-life adventures as a con artist. Abagnale spent years successfully pretending to be an airline pilot, an attorney, a doctor, and more, and hunters must create their own illusions if they want to bag a wily whitetail buck using decoys.

Hunting deer with nontraditional decoys has provided me with countless days of amazement, success, and even laughter. Here are some of my most effective and unusual decoys and why they work.

MOUNTED DOE HEADS AND RUMPS

I first began using nontraditional decoys in the mid-1970s, long before today's wide variety of high-tech decoys were available. Back then, I carried the mounted head or rump of a whitetail doe into the woods. Just for the record, I was careful to only use these

The doe head and rump mounts and the mature doe tail are among the nontraditional decoys I've used effectively over the years. For obvious safety reasons, I never use the mounts unless I'm on private land.

decoys on private land that I leased. Even then, I transported them wrapped in a blaze-orange safety vest. While I enjoyed success with these decoys, they were too cumbersome and heavy to lug around.

Eventually, I traded the mounted versions for the heads and rumps of light Styrofoam deer targets. Deer are just as curious to check them out, and they're a lot easier to carry and set up.

CORN

Early in the 1980s, I began to get more creative with decoys. I still wanted to have the kind of decoy that would make deer investigate, but I wanted it to be small and light enough to carry in my backpack. I began to think about the things that attract deer.

The idea for using fake corn came to me while I was goose hunting in a field. I set out my goose decoys and about a hundred ears of plastic corn. Only minutes after settling into my blind, I noticed a four-point buck walk out of the nearby woodlot. As he passed along the edge of the field, he kept glancing toward my decoys.

At first, I thought he was curious about, or maybe disturbed by, the goose decoys. But then he quickly turned and headed directly into the field, passing some of the decoys and heading right to the plastic ears of corn on the ground. He smelled, mouthed, and even licked one ear. When he was satisfied that it wasn't really food he casually turned and walked away.

I already knew that deer were visually oriented animals, more so than most hunters realize. So it didn't surprise me when the buck was drawn to the yellow corn. Deer are often attracted to food sources simply by sight. It didn't take long for me to start wondering what would happen if I put corn scent on the plastic ears and placed them in the deer woods.

On my next whitetail hunt I placed several scented plastic ears of corn under a tree stand deep in the woods on a mountain behind my house. The nearest cornfield was over a mile away. The first group of deer that passed by were does, yearlings, and fawns. They smelled the corn scent and started to scan the area as they moved toward the fields. Seconds later, they saw the fake corn and made a beeline for it. They licked and mouthed the ears for several minutes before finally deciding they weren't edible. Then they moved off.

An eight-point buck ambled by within a half hour, almost in the does' tracks. And just like the does, he scented the corn before he saw it. My arrow found its mark as he was licking the plastic corn.

I quickly realized that I'd struck decoy gold.

I shot this buck over plastic ears of corn covered in corn scent. This is an unorthodox but highly successful decoy that works virtually anywhere.

APPLES

Over the next winter I thought hard about other decoys that might work as well as the corn. One of the lessons I took away from my experience with corn was that the decoy food source didn't need to grow naturally in the area to be effective.

So I bought several plastic red apples from a craft store and ornament hooks to hang the fake apples from tree limbs. I selected the largest, shiniest, reddest apples I could find to maximize the odds of catching the eyes of passing deer. I then soaked the apples in a commercial apple scent (available in most sporting goods stores) in a large Ziploc bag.

Wearing plastic gutting gloves, I hung some apples from the branches of pine trees near my stand and scattered the remaining apples on the ground. As luck would have it, the first deer down the trail was a shooter buck. He caught sight of the apples seconds before he lifted his nose in the air to wind them. His reaction was immediate and predictable. Although there were no real apple trees within miles, the buck headed directly toward the plastic decoys. I'll never know whether he was going to lick them or not because I shot him at fifteen yards, just as he was starting to examine the apples on the forest floor.

If you don't believe that deer will go out of their way to check out a fake food source placed miles from where it occurs naturally, just try it for yourself. Take some real apples into the deer woods after hunting season is over and scatter them on a well-used trail where apples do not grow naturally. I guarantee you that the deer will see and smell the apples and then stop to eat them.

The same will hold true for your plastic apple or corn decoys. While deer won't be able to eat them, they will be drawn in close enough for a shot.

GRASS

After having so much success with plastic corn and apples, I was confident enough to experiment with other food sources. While perusing a craft store one day for more plastic apples, I found an eight-square-inch section of grass. The grass was about five inches tall and as green as any legume food plot gets in summer. I knew I could use this decoy effectively, but I figured I'd need at least four to six squares. I bought a dozen.

Keep in mind, this stuff is totally worthless when there is still plenty of natural grass available. But when snow covers all the natural foods in the fields and woods, this decoy can be a real magnet.

To make a grass decoy work naturally, you must create the entire illusion. First, buy a bottle of earth scent and a bottle of any type of grass scent (legume works well). Lightly spray the plastic grass with the earth scent, and then apply the grass scent more heavily. Unlike estrus scent, you can't overuse a food scent, but there's still no need to spray on too much. Use just enough so that you can smell it without holding your nose to it.

Leave it overnight in a large Ziploc bag. When you get to your stand, place several of the squares within shooting range. I promise you that the first deer to move through the area will spot the delicious-looking grass sticking out above the snow. Deer always check out a free lunch. It won't take a buck long to figure out it's inedible, but by then he'll be in your sights—and soon in your freezer.

TROLLING FOR BUCKS

My next strategy involved creating a decoy using the natural tail from an adult doe. (Be sure to check your state game laws before using this type of decoy.)

My favorite and most effective nontraditional decoy is a natural deer tail. In fact, I no longer use the doe head or rump because the tail is much easier to carry.

Go to any taxidermist or game processor and ask if they'd mind cutting off the tail and a small piece of hide from the rump of a mature doe. Next, flesh out all the remaining meat and other tissue from the hide. Now salt and cure it.

Break the cartilage at the tip of the tail so that the last few inches are shaped like a question mark. (This is crucial to creating the entire illusion.) Place the tail in the freezer for several months, and then take it out well before deer season. Check to see that no tissue remains and that there is no foul odor. It's okay if it smells of deer hide.

If it needs no further cleaning, make a small hole in the hide through which you can pass a heavy cord. The same type of cord you would use to hoist a firearm into your tree stand is fine; just make sure it's green.

Always take the time to create the full illusion so that the deer is attracted visually and by scent.

Place the deer tail on a stout log about twenty yards from your tree or ground stand. Make sure that the tail isn't in line with where you're posted. (I never use this decoy on posted ground or anytime during opening weekend. I stick to my private farm or to remote areas where I know there are no other hunters.) Place it about thirty-two inches off the ground, which will look natural to any incoming deer. During September and October, sprinkle the deer tail lightly with regular doe urine, not estrus scent.

This decoy tactic is particularly effective for bowhunters. When deer pass out of range you usually have only two options: try to call them back or watch them move off. By twitching the deer tail, you create a powerful enticement to bring a buck or doe all the way in to bow range.

As soon as I get to my stand I hang the tail on the log or branch. After allowing the woods to settle down for the first thirty minutes, I begin to very lightly twitch the tail so that it moves a couple of inches each time I tug gently on the string. Many times—to my surprise, early on—a deer appears out of the brush and slowly walks toward the tail. Obviously, the deer sees the movement from cover and is attracted by it.

Other times, I actually see deer that are out of range, especially during bow season, and I immediately twitch the tail and make a soft social blat in the direction of where the tail is hanging. In almost every case, the buck or doe stops and looks in the direction of the tail and then moves toward it.

This tactic has accounted for dozens of bucks over the years, as well as many, many does.

But the fun with this decoy really begins during the peak of the frenzy period of the rut. (See chapter 10 for more information on this stage of the rut.) Bucks are running helter-skelter around the woods and fields checking for the aroma of estrus scent or actual does in estrus. They abandon their natural caution because their instinct to survive is overpowered by their sex drive. If you're male, you know the feeling. Decisions are transferred from the brain to a lower and less thoughtful organ in the body.

At any rate, the frenzy period is a wonderful time to be in the deer woods. I use the tail a little differently during this time than I did back in September and October.

I start by spraying the tail with some type of doe estrus. I use Love Potion No. 9, but go with whatever product you have confidence in. Don't overuse estrus scent. Too much scent can cause a buck to react negatively. I then place the tail in a Ziploc bag overnight.

The next morning I hang the tail on a branch. Instead of just tugging on the tail to make it move slightly as I did earlier in the season, I gently pull until the tail is hanging straight out from the branch or log to which it's attached. I want the tail to look as if a doe is holding it out and slightly off to one side. As most hunters know, a doe that is ready to be mounted by a buck holds her tail in this position. This is a strong visual signal to all bucks that she is ready, willing, and able—*right now.*

Let's say a buck is across a field or in the woods, roughly a hundred yards upwind of a hot doe's estrus scent. Instead of having to run across the field or through the woods to check the status of her estrus cycle, the buck immediately can see she is ready by the position of her tail. He needs no further incentive to get himself over there in a hurry.

So the tail decoy has a new powerful attraction when it's held straight out on the branch. Once I have the position just right, I gently jig the tail so the very tip flaps. That is why you broke the cartilage—to make the tip of the tail flexible. When a doe is in heat and her tail is straight out, she "flags" the white tip to get the attention of passing bucks. We all know why the bottom of a deer's tail is white, but the tip is also totally white, especially on a doe. Bucks that are far away and upwind can still catch sight of this obvious mating signal.

When using this tactic I've seen bucks throw caution to the wind and run in from long distances to check out what they think is the tail of a hot doe. On at least one occasion, the overwrought buck arrived at the tail and didn't even care that the rest of the "tail" was missing.

Of all my unorthodox decoying tactics, this one has proven itself the most effective. If it's legal in your state, get yourself a doe tail and watch the bucks come running.

MOCK RUBS

Some common-sense decoy tactics are also quite useful. As we all know, rubs play a big role in the world of the whitetail. What some hunters may not realize, though, is that the rub is a lot more than a place to rub off velvet or build up neck muscles.

I made this mock rub about fifteen yards from a natural one. Keep your rubs the same size as, or slightly smaller than, existing rubs. (Kate Fiduccia)

While these two things do occur when a buck rubs a tree, they aren't the most important elements of a rub.

Rubs are also strong olfactory (scent) and visual signposts. A buck rubs trees to establish them as marking posts within its home range and, on occasion, outside its normal territory. It's his way of announcing who he is to does and other bucks, along with what status he holds within the pecking order.

He does this by depositing scent from a variety of glands, and by peeling the bark from the tree or sapling, which is the visual part of the rub. As any deer hunter knows, a rubbed tree can be spotted from quite a distance in the woods or across a field. Bucks and does can pick out this visual signpost from much greater distances than we can, and they're very attracted to them, especially when the rubs are fresh and in a new area.

Every buck goes through the same exact routine before making a new rub or refreshing an old one. As he approaches the tree, he pauses to urinate. While doing so, he squeezes his legs together and presses on a gland within the penal sheath, the preputial gland. This gland releases a powerful aroma that is mixed into the urine. The urine and the scent from the preputial gland run down the buck's legs and pass over the tarsal glands, picking up even more of his unique scent before hitting the ground. (For more information about deer glands, see chapter 15.)

Now he approaches the tree and begins to rub. While doing this he deposits fresh scent from a gland on his forehead, the sebaceous gland. This small gland in the skin secretes a lubricating oily matter, called sebum, into the hair follicles to lubricate the skin and hair. The sebum has a strong aroma that adheres to the bark of the tree.

After the buck makes a few rubs he pauses to lick the tree. He does this so he can deposit another pungent aroma from his arsenal of glands; this one is from the vomeronasal gland, which is located in the roof of his mouth. He also deposits this scent on low-hanging branches or on an accompanying licking stick (a small sapling) that is close to the rubbed tree. This gland helps a buck evaluate the status of a doe's estrus state and her willingness to mate. He checks the odor of a doe's urine by lip curling, or flehming.

All these aromas tell other deer exactly who made the rub. Most hunters are unaware that rubs have multiple users. Many bucks use the rubs of other deer as a way of marking their area and announcing that they were the most recent to pass by.

So how can you use this as a decoy tactic? Go about thirty yards away from a natural rub, and with a small handsaw make a decoy rub facing in the same direction as the natural one. Make the mock rub slightly smaller so you don't spook the buck that made the real rub. If he thinks it was made by the biggest buck in the area, he'll avoid it no matter how big he is.

Now place just one or two drops of forehead scent on the tree. (Use more, and you risk making the scent too powerful.) Next, place some buck urine in and around the area. If you can find a commercially made scent for the vomeronasal gland, you can use that too, but only a small drop or two.

Now measure your mock rub. It should be only an inch or two smaller than the natural rub. Over the next couple of days that you hunt your mock rub, you may or may not see a buck. Don't become disheartened if no deer show up. A buck may have visited the site when you weren't there. In order to find this out, measure your rub again. If it's larger than it was originally you can be sure that another buck has been there working on it. This should give you enough confidence to continue to hunt it for a few more days. If you don't see the buck during that time, make a new rub somewhere else.

When you finally do attract a buck to your decoy rub, I predict you'll describe it something like this: As the buck approached the new rub, he stopped in his tracks. He hesitated for about a minute before moving toward the decoy rub. When he was within ten yards or so, he stopped again, squeezed his rear legs together, and urinated. Then he approached and rubbed his antlers on the tree as he pressed his forehead against the trunk. Then he paused and licked where he just rubbed. He repeated this several times. Next he licked or mouthed an overhanging branch or a licking stick and casually walked off, sometimes stopping to urinate as he went.

Mock rubs have helped me take a lot of bucks. What makes this such a good decoy? The buck's natural behavior to investigate rubs made by other bucks, especially new rubs. He has no choice. It is his instinctive duty. If he doesn't see or smell you hiding nearby, he'll definitely check out your rub.

This decoy tactic can also be adapted to scrapes, as all the same olfactory and visual principles apply.

THE ACORN CROP

I began discussing the following decoy tactic in my deer hunting seminars twenty-three years ago. Since then, many other outdoor communicators have picked up on it. The tactic is simple but highly effective. If you own your own land or lease it you can do this on several mast trees, especially white oaks spread throughout the woods. If you hunt public land, you may want to try it on only one or two trees.

Find a mature tree within a group of mast-producing trees. Then fertilize the tree twice a year, once in spring and again in fall, with a standard 10-10-10 mix. You can plant spikes in holes or spread granulated fertilizer on top of the ground. I don't recommend the latter if you're doing this on public ground, though, because you'll give yourself away to other hunters. Place the fertilizer at the drip line, which is the branch farthest away from the trunk of the tree.

The first year you do this the tree will produce bigger acorns. The second season they will be even bigger, and they'll stay on the branches longer before falling. In the third year—and in all subsequent years, as long as you continue to fertilize the tree— the acorns it produces will be bigger, sweeter, and hold on longer than those on other trees. If you don't believe me, taste the acorns for yourself in the second year. They'll still taste bitter, although less bitter than other acorns nearby.

Fertilizing select mast trees twice a year will help them consistently produce acorns like these, even in years when natural production is low or absent. (Ted Rose)

Your trees will soon become a magnet for deer, turkey, and black bear. And unless you give their location away, no one will know but you. Deer will come to your fertilized trees first, knowing they produce more and tastier food than other vegetation in their range. It's a terrific decoy tactic.

This tactic also works on other natural vegetation. You can fertilize and prune wild grapevines, crab apple or persimmon trees, and a variety of other trees and shrubs that produce fruit and nuts that deer like to eat.

I've used the unusual decoy tactics covered above with great success over the years. Try them with confidence, and they will surely work for you. But don't ignore manufactured decoys just because my unorthodox methods are effective. I use commercial decoys successfully as well. I didn't give these decoys much attention here because manufacturers and outdoor writers have already produced quite a bit of information about these traditional methods.

Ted Rose

Chapter
14

GETTING TO KNOW DEER

A lot of hunters skim over chapters like this in hunting books, but knowing your quarry inside and out will make you a better hunter. You may be surprised how often the information below comes into play when you're planning a hunt, stalking after a track, or—as I have seen countless times—when calling or rattling to mature bucks.

NATURAL HISTORY

The white-tailed deer began its evolutionary journey millions of years ago with the Tertiary and Quaternary cervids; probably right alongside man's ancestor, Australopithecus. During this early period of development, the Eocene period, it was grouped in the order of Artiodactlys—even-toed ungulates, mammals whose body weight is maintained by the third and fourth metapodials (toes).

Many species within the deer family group died out during the Miocene epoch. Other members of the order went on to become the breeding stock of today's Artiodactyls, which include the Suina (pigs, peccaries, and hippopotamuses) and the Ruminantia (the cud-chewers).

Modern-day ruminants most often have two "functional" toes, metapodials melded as cannon bones, complex selenodont molars, upper incisors that are smaller or missing, canines that are inadequate or at best slightly enlarged in males, and compound stomachs. The current Cervidae family includes the white-tailed deer, mule deer, black-tailed deer, elk, moose, reindeer, caribou, and others.

In North and Central America there are about thirty subspecies of white-tailed deer. In the U.S. and Canada there are some seventeen subspecies. The major huntable subspecies include the white-tailed deer (*Odocoileus virginianus*), the Columbia black-tailed deer (*Odocoileus hemionus columbianus*), the Sitka black-tailed deer (*Odocoileus hemionus sitkensis*), and the Coues' white-tailed deer (*Odocoileus virginianus couesi*). Although taxonomists revel in arguments about the total number of definable subspecies, most hunters across the country need only know they are chasing *Odocoileus virginianus*.

Many hunters are interested in collecting at least one of each of these deer. In fact, Safari Club International (SCI), Boone & Crockett (B&C), and other record-keeping organizations have separate trophy categories for each subspecies. They also offer awards to hunters who bag one trophy-caliber buck in each category (the "grand slam" of deer).

There is little doubt that the whitetail is the most popular big game animal across North America. It provides about fifteen million deer hunters a challenging recreational opportunity, an alternate food source, and a chance to hang a trophy on the den wall.

This is also the most widely distributed deer on the continent. It is found from the Deep South swamps of Florida to the coniferous forests of Maine, along the river bottoms of the Rockies, in the shrub-and-cactus deserts of Texas, and in the frigid northern mountains of Alberta, Canada. And its range continues to grow each year. In fact, whitetails are now quite common in the Rocky Mountain states of Idaho, Montana, Wyoming, and Colorado.

Many guides in the Rockies and western Canada can testify to the fact that the white-tailed deer is methodically expanding its range from the thickly vegetated river bottoms and drainages to less hospitable mountainous areas or arid plains, where food and cover isn't as readily available. Some biologists believe that the dwindling numbers of mule deer across the West are directly related to the expansion of the whitetail's range.

No matter where the whitetail calls home, it easily learns to adapt to the conditions and terrain. It has learned to thrive within city limits, to tolerate and adapt to land-use programs (baseball fields, golf courses, parks, and county picnic areas), and to endure shrinking habitat due to the construction of suburban malls and other developments.

In fact, the whitetail actually benefits from many types of human encroachment. As mature forests are cut down, second-growth trees, grasslands, and pastures are created—ideal habitat for the whitetail, which prefers edges and new growth. The new, succulent, tender growth is highly sought after by deer. All this new growth helps increase the land's carrying capacity for whitetails. So despite how much we hunt the whitetail or alter its environment, it seems to continuously adapt throughout its range.

Whitetails in different geographic regions often exhibit differences in physical characteristics: hair color, overall body size and weight, height and length, and antler size.

I learned this firsthand in 1987 when I shot my first south Texas buck, a fourteen-pointer, in Sarita, Texas. The 6½-year-old buck's antlers scored 167 5/8 B&C points, yet the deer field dressed at only 98 pounds. Many people who see the head mount of this buck often remark that it looks like a doe fitted with a large

I shot this fourteen-point buck in Sarita, Texas. Note the small ears and face and short hair common on all south Texas and Mexican whitetails. Despite the trophy headgear, this buck dressed out at just 98 pounds. (Kate Fiduccia)

rack. The ears are much smaller than those on its northern cousins, the hair is much thinner and almost velvet-like to the touch, the neck long and sleek, and the head small.

The buck was killed fairly close to the border with Mexico. Deer of that region in Texas are classified as *O. v. texanus*, as are Mexico's deer. Closely related to this subspecies are other small deer like the Coues' deer in the Southwest and the Key deer in the Florida Keys. These subspecies are all smaller than other whitetails found in North America.

These diminutive whitetails have evolved this way in response to their environment. The areas in which they live are hot and arid for at least half the year and fairly warm in other months, so the evolutionary process has forced some necessary adjustments. They are smaller in overall body size — Key deer rarely exceed twenty-eight inches at the shoulder and more than eighty pounds live weight—and the hair on their coats is not as long as other deer. Even the ears, face, and tails are smaller than on other whitetails.

Why? Adaptation. These deer don't have to endure severe winter climates. The typical "northern" body characteristics would hinder deer that live in these hot, dry areas of the country. A larger body would mean the deer would have to take in more food and water to fuel, nourish, and cool itself. And hides with thicker, longer hair wouldn't disperse body heat as effectively.

Conversely, deer living in the cold winter climates typical of northern Michigan, Minnesota, and Maine (*O. v. borealis*) or Saskatchewan, Alberta, and British Columbia (*O. v. ochrourus*) have larger bodies and thicker coats than southern bucks. Although the larger body requires more food, it can sustain itself with greater fat reserves. These reserves also provide insulation against the cold.

The subspecies of deer residing in the northernmost portions or latitudes of the country are mostly *O. v. borealis* and *O. v. dacotensis.* Nature has genetically engineered these white-tailed deer to be the largest subspecies, with most specimens standing forty inches high at the shoulder. In comparison, the whitetails of Texas stand about thirty-four to thirty-six inches at the shoulder.

In the northern regions of North America, the length of an adult male deer may reach ninety-five inches from the tip of the nose to the tail. Whitetails found in the central U.S. generally average around seventy-two inches in length, and southwestern deer run only about fifty-five inches.

The largest white-tailed buck ever recorded was a Minnesota deer taken in 1926. The buck dressed out at a whopping 402 pounds and had an estimated live weight of 511 pounds. Another buck taken in the northern tier of neighboring Wisconsin in 1924 had a dressed weight of 386 pounds, which gave it an estimated live weight of 491 pounds. Even today, it isn't unusual for mature bucks to dress out at 200 to 250 pounds, especially in Maine, Saskatchewan, or the Adirondack Mountains of New York.

The antler size and dimensions of mature whitetail bucks depend mostly on three factors: age, diet, and genetic inheritance. Geographic conditions also come into play to a degree.

THE "EYES" HAVE IT

It's no longer a secret that deer can see a wide range of colors, at least to some degree. This was discovered as early as 1977, at the U.S. Department of Agriculture's veterinary laboratory in College Station, Texas. Several doctors examined the eyes of anesthetized deer with electron microscopes. They quickly noticed that the deer's eyes had a large number of nerve endings called "rods," but this wasn't a new discovery. Biologists have long known that rods are light receptors and are present in many animal species that are primarily nocturnal. So it was understandable that deer should have a large number of rods to help them feed and move in low light and to spot danger in total darkness.

What did surprise the biologists was the fact that deer's eyes also had a large number of "cones," which are color receptors. When the scientists stimulated the eyes with flashes of light covering the entire color spectrum they reacted to the different lights almost in the same way human eyes react, proving that deer do, indeed, recognize colors.

In another study done in Michigan, biologists used deer in a pen that were fully alert and in a natural environment. The biologists used conditioning techniques that allowed the deer to receive rewards of food when they made the right responses to certain colors and no food when they didn't. The experiment soon revealed that the deer could distinguish both long and short wavelength colors. What shocked the biologists, though, was that the deer made correct responses to all the different colors 95 percent of the time.

A whitetail's eye only needs an eighth of the available light a human's eye needs to see in the dark. The white hair directly under the eyes of the whitetail also helps it see better at night, as this hair reflects more light into the eye in low-light conditions.

Unbelievably, whitetails can see at least 310 degrees of the 360 degrees in a full circle, and at least 50 degrees of the 310 degrees can be seen in binocular vision.

White-tailed deer also have depth perception and have evolved to quickly detect motion. The eyes of a deer have monocular vision to each eye and binocular vision to the front, giving a wide field of view. The design of the orbit (the bony socket in

A deer's eyes are its weakest line of defense, but they're still a force hunters should respect. There is an ongoing controversy about whether or not deer can see color. (Ted Rose)

which the eye lies) and the size of the retina (the sensory membrane that lines the eye and is connected to the brain by the optic nerve) allow all ruminant animals to see back along their flanks and to detect objects behind them.

One of the most controversial aspects regarding a deer's eyesight revolves around its ability to detect ultraviolet (UV) light. Many hunters are concerned about the effect UV light has on "untreated" hunting clothing under low-light conditions. Much of the information available on the subject is packed with technical data and misleading graphs detailing how animals, particularly deer, are able to detect hunters wearing garments, including blaze-orange and camouflaged clothing, containing UV brighteners.

Although these articles strongly suggest deer do see UV light and colors, exactly how animals interpret them is still debatable. In one article I read about UV light, the author began by stating, "Laboratory experiments prove that deer see many things we cannot see, especially ultraviolet light at the blue-white end of the color spectrum." As far as I know, white isn't a color and isn't on the spectrum.

Let's look at the facts. It's true that most nocturnal animals can see as well in the dark as they can during daylight hours. They are able to see better in total darkness and, supposedly, best under low-light conditions. When the sun sets, a deer's pupils open wider to admit more light. The rods, which are dominant within the eye, are extremely sensitive to light, particularly dim light.

Human eyes have a filter that blocks out UV light, while deer are without this filter.

But the question remains: Can deer and other game animals detect enough UV light reflected from a hunter's camo clothing at dawn and dusk to require us to change our hunting strategies or clothing?

Some people think so. A manufacturer of a product called UV Killer was the first to address the issue of UV light and clothing. In a booklet called "How Game Animals See," the manufacturer supported his findings with research compiled by a vision scientist at the University of California. According to the booklet, hunters who wear camouflaged clothing manufactured with, or enhanced by, UV brighteners are using camo that "has been working against [them]."

The theory is that animals detect the UV light reflected from clothing and are spooked by it. But with UV Killer (which is actually another dye that neutralizes brighteners in clothing), sportsmen can eliminate UV reflection from their clothing and be less visible to game.

Let's assume for a moment that the manufacturer's UV theory is correct. These ultraviolet brighteners come from standard detergents used to wash clothing. So if a sportsman washes his clothes in regular detergent there's a greater chance his detergent, and hence his clothing, has ultraviolet brighteners in it. However, for the last fifteen to twenty years deer hunters have been advised to wash their clothing in an unscented detergent or brown soap to control scent. Most of these "hunter's soaps" contain basic cleaning agents that are free from ultraviolet brighteners. So even if UV brighteners really are a problem, most hunters are already wearing camo clothing that is "safe."

At best, the ability of deer to detect and react to UV light reflected from clothing seems to be greatly exaggerated. Leading scientists involved in extensive vision research just don't support the claim that animals, especially mammals, detect UV light as being brighter than any other light they see. Since no documented research (using accepted psychophysiological methods specifically for deer) has been performed regarding deer's ability to detect UV light, little can be said to prove they can actually detect UV reflection from clothes.

John Coulbourn, president of Coulbourn Instruments, who has a degree in behavioral psychology and zoology, stated the following, "The notion that deer see ultraviolet wavelengths with significantly greater sensitivity than other mammals (including humans) is unlikely." Coulbourn Instruments is primarily involved in manufacturing behavioral and physiological test instruments for drug and toxicology research. They have completed extensive studies regarding vision in animals.

Coulbourn also feels that the pictures often displayed in hunting advertisements and articles are pointless. "No organism with a single lens eye could simultaneously focus on red and green and ultraviolet [as the pictures portray]," he noted. "Either it would see an ultraviolet image and a blurred red-green haze or the reverse. Not being able to focus on an image or even detect target movement in this region of the spectrum means evolution would not select for this capability.

"Mammals (in fact, most vertebrates) that have color sensitivity are similar to humans, and any deviations from our green-centered sensitivity tend to be to the far red, the opposite end of the spectrum from violet. This is especially true for nocturnally active animals."

He went on to explain how deer's vision is different from our own: "While we concentrate on image formation and pattern-form discrimination, deer are more responsive to movement or target velocity across the retina. This is a common adaptation in prey animals that are attacked by swiftly moving predators."

Dr. Silas White, professor of psychology at Muhlenberg College, also finds the concept of deer being able to detect clear images from ultraviolet reflection difficult to believe.

"In vertebrate studies performed thus far," he says, "in no case does there appear to be much, if any, sensitivity to radiant energy in the UV end of the spectrum. This militates strongly against UV reflections being perceived as brighter than other wavelengths . . . It is unlikely that, if UV were indeed an adequate stimulus, which is doubtful, deer or humans would be capable of perceiving a crisp image resulting from reflections of such disparate wavelengths as those in the typical deer woods background and UV reflections."

And it isn't just scientists outside the hunting fraternity that have doubts about the so-called "revolutionary" findings related to UV light. Many seasoned outdoor professionals also don't think deer can interpret reflections from UV light. Glenn Cole, a wildlife manager for the New York Department of Environmental Conservation, has hunted whitetails for over thirty years. "The hard facts to support what an animal does or does not see under low-light conditions are just not available," he notes. "All the scientific literature I have read says deer see in shades of gray. I have not seen any scientific material to the contrary. I can honestly say that any deer that has spooked from seeing me was reacting to movement or scent, and not because my camo clothing was reflecting UV light."

Let's take a closer look at Coulbourn's point that nature has granted all animals that are predated upon with vision that is super-sensitive to motion rather than color. For instance, a rabbit that is feeding with eyes focused downward is able to quickly detect a hawk approaching because the hawk's shadow triggers an instinctive response. The rabbit instantly reacts by hunkering down, pinning its ears back, and darting off. A deer reacts much the same way when it spots something that suggests danger.

Virtually all deer hunters have witnessed this behavior. The deer remains motionless or cautiously approaches the anomaly in its environment. With a single movement from the hunter (or predator), however, the deer flees.

In all my years of hunting I've never had an animal become frightened or run away because it spotted UV light reflected from my clothing. In fact, on many occasions I've had deer actually approach me. I've done intensive research with whitetails in the wild and at deer research preserve facilities, and it has been my experience that the overwhelming majority of deer that I've spooked in these environments caught my scent or detected my movement. Clothing color didn't really factor into these encounters.

Think about your own hunting experiences. How many times have you had deer, or other game animals, very close to you while wearing so-called untreated hunting clothing? Many hunters have had a deer stare them down, trying to decipher what it was looking at, and then decide that what it saw wasn't a threat. These deer often start feeding again or calmly walk away. If they detected a glowing UV light, would they really react this way?

Other than eliminating human scent, camouflage has been the most important factor in my getting close to deer undetected. I have harvested and videotaped many bucks while they were staring directly at me, unable to figure out what they were looking at. And many of my hunting companions through the years have told me about deer that came within touching distance, despite the fact that the hunters wore untreated camouflage clothing.

Until there is more viable and conclusive evidence about how deer react to ultraviolet light reflected from camo clothing I intend to continue hunting in untreated clothing. This isn't because I take special pleasure in proving the UV theory wrong, but rather because I don't want to change my long-time winning formula. At least for now, the UV reflection issue is mostly bogus.

The most important thing a hunter needs to keep in mind is that a deer's eyes, just like those of all prey animals, are designed to pick up the slightest of movements.

ON THE HOOF

The whitetail's prehistoric ancestors had five toes on each foot. Over time, this proved to be a disadvantage for deer; it hindered their ability to run fast enough to escape predators. As deer evolved, the other three toes changed. The first toe completely vanished, while the other two slowly began to regress or atrophy. Today we know these two toes as dewclaws. The two remaining toes slowly developed into the main toenails, or hooves, that we see on modern deer.

The whitetail's hoof has also adapted well to the firm surfaces of woods, fields, and the like, although it's not particularly useful on the ice of frozen lakes or ponds. When a deer falls on ice it may never be able to get back up. Many deer have died from exhaustion after falling on lake ice and struggling for hours to regain their balance.

The hoof is also used by bucks and does as a defensive weapon against predators. The deer stands on its hind legs and flails its forelegs at the intruder. The blows can be powerful enough to crush the skull of a wolf, coyote, domestic dog, or even a man. Even a glancing blow to the body can inflict a deep, tearing wound.

Does typically use this form of antagonistic behavior with other deer only when all other types of aggressive body language and vocalizations, along with light foreleg kicks, have failed to get the desired results. They may also use their hooves to keep other mature deer from the food sources of their fawns. And does often strike out at fawns and yearlings as a disciplinary action, or when they want to prevent them from eating a food source, especially during a hard winter. Bucks use their hooves as additional weapons when they fight other bucks during the rut.

A deer's front hooves are usually larger than its rear hooves, and deer are knock-kneed. This accounts for why the outside of the hoof is generally larger than the inside on each foot. Deer are more inclined to walk on the inside lobe, leaving the unique angle we see when we look at their tracks.

As I mentioned in the tracking section, you're making life hard for yourself if you try to judge the sex of a deer solely by its track. Use common sense, and factor in other sign left by deer to tell if you're following a buck. If you've ever heard one of my seminars or read any of my other books you know that I'm a strong believer that common sense is a major factor in consistent hunting success.

YOU CAN'T "HIDE" FROM THE FACTS

A whitetail's coat comes in many different shades—and in a few instances different color phases—depending on where it lives. Primary colors are hereditary, such as melanism (all black), piebalds (patches of white and brown or all-white with brown eyes), or albinism (all white with pink eyes). In general, a deer's coat is a mix of black hair, a few shades of brown hair, and white hair.

This coat is an evolutionary thermoregulatory marvel of nature. In summer, it is reddish in color and made up of solid, straight, thin hairs with no undercoat. The thin coat helps keep deer cool during the heat of summer, although it offers little protection from biting insects. Surprisingly, the summer coat actually includes more hairs per square inch than the winter coat.

The hair of a whitetail's winter undercoat is soft, thin, and kinky. The outer coat hair is hollow, longer, and thicker. Each hollow hair is filled with air cells, offering the whitetail two layers of superb insulation. You can see just how good a deer's winter coat insulates it by watching deer during a snowstorm or on a frosty morning. A deer loses so little body heat through the top of its coat in winter that the frost or snow clings to its back without

This buck's snow-covered hide demonstrates how its hollow hair retains warmth even in the coldest of temperatures. (Ted Rose)

melting. In fact, snow falling on any part of the upper body won't melt as long as the hair is standing on end.

But when the hair is laid flat against the body, snow melts rapidly. Any hunter who has come across a deer bed can attest to the fact that the snow in the bed has melted. It does so because any body heat that escapes is trapped beneath the animal by the snow and earth.

The hair on the front of the chest (brisket) points forward, while all other hair is directed back or down. It is also important for hunters to know that the hair on various sections of the whitetail's body differs in color and texture. On many occasions I've used information on hair color and texture to determine exactly where I shot a whitetail that ran off, especially when I'm bowhunting. It provides critical tracking clues for following up wounded deer. (See chapter 5 for more information on identifying body hair.)

DEER "EAR" IT ALL

There's an old saying that when a leaf falls to the forest floor the turkey sees it, the bear smells it, and the whitetail hears it. The whitetail's ears are exceptionally sensitive and quickly detect any out-of-the-ordinary sound within its habitat.

But the whitetail doesn't spend its days ducking and running from every sound it hears. If it did, it wouldn't have time to feed, drink, or rest. Deer quickly learn to recognize all the different noises in their environment. They hear songbirds chattering all day; turkeys scratching leaves aside for food, purring, gobbling, flying up and down from roosting sites; squirrels barking, chattering, and running through the forest. The wind causes trees to creak, breaks branches, and snaps off limbs. In other words, the woods are anything but quiet.

Add to those natural sounds the noise of farm machinery, vehicles on roads, hikers, campers, and voices from nearby homes, and you can see that deer must process a wide variety of sounds every day of their lives. They learn from birth which sounds are normal and which aren't. When their ears pick up something unusual, they react immediately.

A deer's ears play a major role in its survival. They can be rotated together or independently to pick up any sound that might represent danger.

A deer's ears are particularly adept at detecting high-pitched sounds projecting up to 30,000 cycles per second. (Human ears can only pick up 16,000 cycles per second.) Each ear has an amazingly large area, about twenty-four square inches of surface from which to gather sounds. Deer can turn their ears in a 180-degree arc, and they regularly swivel each ear to determine if anything unfamiliar is occurring in their surroundings and to monitor the whereabouts and behavior of other animals, especially predators.

Once they detect danger, deer begin a three-step process of recognition, identification, and response. Sometimes this process sparks an immediate flee response and sometimes the deer doesn't appear to react at all. It simply returns to whatever it was doing before it heard the sound.

A whitetail's reactions are often related to the variable distances at which it detects particular noises. This phenomenon is known as the Doppler effect. As a noise gets closer, it seems to become louder because the frequency of the sound wave seems higher. When the noise passes, the pitch begins to drop, getting lower as the source of the noise moves farther and farther away until it can no longer be heard.

Because the neural channels linking a deer's ears to its brain are tuned in to much higher pitched sounds than we're capable of hearing, deer tend to overreact to noises close to them. This point has been brought home to hunters time and time again. You're watching a small herd of deer feeding near your stand, and to your surprise they don't react at all to a distant gunshot, or the faint sound of a farmer's voice, or even a car horn on a nearby road. But step on a twig, cough, or make a deer call and the whole herd instantly scatters in all directions.

The great contradiction, however, is that deer don't bolt from every single noise close by—sometimes resulting in their demise. If they can't place the sound instantly, they often remain still until they can.

What this all boils down to is that although we're incapable of eliminating all sounds while hunting, we'll see more deer if we keep our sounds to a minimum. If you step on a branch and it snaps or if you make some other loud sound, just freeze. Wait a few minutes while carefully watching and listening for deer. If you don't see or hear anything, continue on your way. If you do spot a deer, watch how it holds its ears and you'll be able to better predict what it's thinking and what it's about to do. Body language can provide you with a lot of information.

KNOW THE NOSE

A deer's sense of smell is often its primary defense system. And this makes perfect sense, as biologists have documented that the olfactory center of a deer's brain, which absorbs the odor molecules constantly being monitored, is at least 10,000 times more developed than ours. Deer are even capable of distinguishing between several different odors at one time.

The nose aids deer in defining exactly who's who in the deer world on an individual basis. And it not only locates food, but also determines if it's going to be palatable enough to eat. Of course, the nose also detects danger and helps bucks locate receptive does in estrus.

The olfactory sense of a deer is even keener than a bloodhound's, making it the most reliable survival sense. This buck is using his nose to determine the exact state of estrus in a nearby doe. (Ted Rose)

I firmly believe that the deer's sense of smell is its key to survival, and the hunter's key to success in bagging whitetails. To be a consistently successful deer hunter you must bust a buck's ability to use its nose against you. Do so, and you've "busted" the buck.

Each nostril in a deer's nose is lined with epithelium, a cellular tissue composed of mucous membranes and sensory nerve endings. When kept moist by the deer's tongue and the internal tissue itself, the epithelium picks up odors much better. The amount of membranous cellular tissue lining a human nostril is about an 8,000th of the skin's total surface. But in deer it covers an eightieth of the skin's total surface, roughly the same as in dogs.

Obviously, because a deer's nose has more epithelium membrane tissue than a human's (in proportion to total skin surface), it is far better at sensing odors. Although deer can detect odors from as far away as three-quarters of a mile or more, anything picked up at this distance is usually dispersed enough to have little impact. Many biologists believe that a whitetail has to be within fifty to one hundred yards of the source of an odor to have a noticeable reaction. Of course, wind currents affect this general range to a degree.

For hunters, the important thing to remember about a deer's sense of smell is to keep your odor out of its nose! Do so, and you will see and bag more deer.

THE STOMACH

As ruminants, all whitetails have a four-chambered stomach. Each of these chambers is shaped differently, has a different lining, and serves a different and specific function. And each compartment is capable of holding only a certain amount of food.

The rumen, a digestive or fermentation compartment unique to ruminants, lies on top of the intestines. It consists of small papillae varying from ⅜ to ½ inch in length. These look very similar to small lengths of spaghetti, and there are 1,600 to the square inch. The rumen's primary function is to store unchewed food, as much as two gallons of material. It allows the deer to swallow food in large chunks.

A deer eats with its head down, limiting its visual range and leaving it more vulnerable to predators. But its rumen allows the deer to quickly swallow its food in large chunks and then retreat to a safe area of cover. Fatty acids ferment the food, which the deer regurgitates, chews more thoroughly—called cud-chewing—and swallows again.

The second compartment of the deer's stomach is known as the reticulum. It resembles a honeycomb and is about the size of a large orange. The reticulum forces liquid into the rumen, picking up small food particles that are carried back to this compartment and then on to the third chamber, the omasum.

The omasum primarily serves as a dehydrator. It removes excess water from the food. This section has about forty-five to fifty flaps of different sizes that strain the food as it passes through. This is where digestion really begins to take place.

Finally, the food moves on to the abomasum, the fourth compartment. The abomasum secretes enzymes that complete the digestive process. The abomasum is similar to the stomach of non-ruminants in that it is smooth and sleek.

A deer has about sixty to seventy feet of intestines. All unabsorbed foods are gathered here and passed out in the form of excrement. In an adult deer it takes about twenty-four to thirty-six hours for food to be eaten, digested, and passed out as dung.

Ted Rose

Chapter
15

EXTERNAL GLANDS

The deer of North America have been studied more than any other game animal. Since the early 1900s, we have made tremendous gains in understanding behavioral habits and the physiological makeup of these animals. Still, a lot of mysteries remain unsolved.

The external glands of deer aren't a new topic of study. Many biologists have written about their functions and uses. All deer possess the same basic external glands, but gland size on the different species of deer is a factor to consider both taxonomically and physiologically.

The major external glands include the preorbital, interdigital, tarsal, and metatarsal. These glands play a significant role in the life of deer, but they represent only a fraction of a deer's complex glandular anatomy. New biological findings have revealed a few other glands that deer use to mark signposts. These include the vomeronasal, forehead, and penal-sheath glands.

The information presented here includes some facts and some assumptions, as it's difficult to precisely identify all the purposes of each gland. New information concerning glandular activity among deer continues to be published each year. We'll probably never know all the reasons deer do what they do, but with more studies and new findings the gap is slowly closing.

THE METATARSAL GLAND

The metatarsal gland is located on the outer hind leg between the toes and the heel. It isn't well understood, and is thought to be atrophying. All deer have these glands from birth (one on each hind leg).

Many wildlife biologists suggest that gland size, in some cases, can have taxonomic (classification) value between species. The mule deer has the largest metatarsal glands, followed by the black-tailed deer and the white-tailed deer.

Although smaller than on other deer species, this gland is clearly visible on a whitetail. It is surrounded by a light, tannish

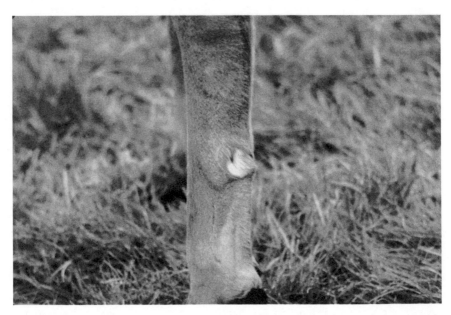

It is widely believed that whitetails no longer need the metatarsal gland, which has evidently begun to atrophy.

circle of hair set against the more dominant reddish-brown or gray colors on the coat. A closer examination of the gland reveals a rib-shaped spot lacking hair.

The metatarsal gland is not a true external gland because it lacks a surface opening and duct. The metatarsals, actually located below the skin surface, are technically known as sebaceous (sweat) and sudoriferous (scent-producing) glands. The latter gland secretes very small amounts of scent, and its purpose has not yet been proven conclusively, so knowledge of its physiology is minimal.

Some biologists speculate that when a deer lies down the metatarsal glands rub the ground and leave a scent. Another possibility is that the metatarsal gland could be a rudimentary vestigial gland that had a more significant purpose earlier in the deer's evolution. Something similar occurred with the dewclaws, which are remnants of what used to be functional toes.

THE TARSAL GLAND

The tarsal gland is a true external gland located inside each hind leg at the foot/heel junction, and it's present at birth in both sexes. Through years of research, biologists have discovered many relevant facts about this gland. In fact, we know more about the tarsal than any other gland. Clearly visible on all three deer species, the tarsal gland plays an important role in reproductive activities, as well as in social dominance and communication.

The tarsal glands are a deer's most important scent glands. They are concealed in hair and measure about four inches in diameter. The hairs associated with the gland are capable of standing on end or flaring out when an unusual or excitable situation arises, putting the deer on guard. When the deer is in an excited state, the hairs can be seen at fairly long distances. And the gland releases scent that clings to the hairs and acts partly as a warning signal to nearby deer.

Wildlife biologist Dietland Mueller-Schwarze states that the active olfactory components in the tarsal gland are lactones. He notes that lactones are both age and sex specific and that the hairs used to deposit the urine and scent (pheromone) mixture are termed "osmetrichia." These lipid-covered hairs are specialized scent hairs.

During the mating season, males, females, and fawns rub-urinate on the tarsal glands for several reasons. Bucks do it as a

The tarsal glands of this buck are in prime condition. The surrounding hair is puffed out and full of urine and glandular scent, and the dark color demonstrates that he's in full rut. (Ted Rose)

means of displaying social dominance. Males smell each other's tarsal glands to determine ranking in the herd. Females rub for self-identification, and fawns depend partly on this when they become separated from does. Fawns also rub-urinate, possibly for identification purposes.

The research of L. W. Bouckhout revealed that socially dominant males rub-urinate more frequently than males of lesser dominance. Other research concluded that the odor of tarsal glands is stronger in dominant males due to the frequency of urination. Young males and females have been known to lick their tarsal glands after rub-urination more than older males. This act is thought to remove scent, perhaps as an expression of lesser dominance.

Deer hunters should know that the tarsal gland is associated only externally with deer. Removal of the gland prior to field dressing or meat cutting is necessary only if a hunter feels he will come in contact with the glands. If contact isn't made, the gland won't spoil or ruin the flavor of the meat.

THE INTERDIGITAL GLAND

The interdigital gland is located between the toes of each foot on both sexes of deer. Functional from birth, these glands emit a unique odor each time a deer takes a step, allowing deer to track one another. The interdigital gland is covered with hair and not readily spotted with the naked eye. Close examination reveals a duct, or opening, between the toes, visible only when the toes are spread and the hair parted. The largest interdigital glands are found on white-tailed deer.

Bucks and does use the scent differently. Females rely on it to track their young, while males use it to follow females during the rut.

An animal's ability to follow only one particular scent among many others is one of nature's most amazing accomplishments. Many kinds of wildlife, especially females and their offspring, can distinguish an individual's scent no matter how many animals are in an area or how many scents there are to differentiate. Since deer rely primarily on scent for positive identification, this gland seems especially important.

THE PREORBITAL GLAND

Located below the eyes on all deer, the preorbital is another gland we don't fully understand. The gland has a small canal or duct from which tiny amounts of scent trickle out. Easily visible, the preorbital is thought to be a scent marker. It is largest in mule deer.

One theory claims that deer use the gland more or less based on habitat. White-tailed and black-tailed deer would probably

The preorbital gland is located in the lower corner of the eye. It lets the deer's brain know when daylight is getting shorter or longer, which controls the timing of the rut.

make best use of this gland since they inhabit areas of dense vegetation, where there are plenty of shrubs and trees on which to rub scent. On the other hand, mule deer inhabit open plains where there is little vegetation to rub against.

But it seems unusual that a marking gland would be so near the eye since it is such a vulnerable area. Twigs and other forest debris could impair vision if the animal were to unknowingly rub near sharp objects.

Another possibility is that the doe uses the gland to smear some of her own scent on her young through nuzzling. This may be beneficial for locating a fawn that has wandered out of the doe's sight.

Epilogue

The most important element in a deer hunting success is to believe in yourself and your hunting skills. Self-doubt causes hunters to lose more opportunities to shoot bucks than any other reason. You must enter the woods knowing—not thinking or hoping—that you will see a buck that day. Doubt your stand selection, and you might as well have stayed home. Doubt your ability when calling, rattling, decoying, or with any of the unorthodox tactics covered in this book, and you will have less success. It's that simple.

If you aren't fully focused on the job at hand, you also seriously reduce your chances of bringing a deer home. You must keep your head in the game.

Let's say you've been sitting in your stand for a few hours. If you're not paying full attention during that time you may not hear the subtle grunt of a buck passing by in the cover or glimpse the white speck of antlers glistening in the sunlight or see a sapling rocking back and forth as a buck rubs it. It only takes a few seconds for a mature buck to sneak by your stand undetected.

Thoughts about work, unfinished chores you have at home, or bills you need to pay must be set aside so that you can note every sight, sound, and smell around your stand. Miss any of these signals and you might be missing potential opportunities to spot and bag your buck.

The next time you go deer hunting promise yourself that you won't question whether or not the site you chose is a good one. Remain there for the next few hours and be confident that you will see deer. If you stay in one spot longer than that, you'll lose concentration and confidence.

Pay close attention to every natural sound you hear. You'll be amazed at how many there are when you focus on listening. Most hunters have never heard a buck grunt or a doe blat; either they don't know what to listen for or their mind is on something other than picking up each and every natural sound in the woods.

Even when you hear a turkey purr, study your surroundings carefully. If a crow or squirrel cries out a warning, concentrate intently on the nearby cover. It you think you hear a branch snap or a slight shuffle of leaves, always assume it's an approaching buck and focus all your senses to that area. (And for you newcomers, that doesn't mean looking through your scope to identify the noise. Always know your target before placing it in your sights.)

You must be ready to react instantly to a buck that is trying to sneak through the woods. If you spot what looks like the ear, nose, eye, or other body part, expect it to be a deer and study it carefully in your binoculars. You'll be surprised at how many times it really is a deer.

And don't be afraid to use a deer call. Not all noises in the woods scare deer. There are good noises and bad noises. Good noises are deer calls, antler rattling, and under the right conditions, shuffling leaves, snapping twigs, and shaking saplings. Bucks and does make these sounds naturally, and they can all attract deer when used correctly.

Avoid bad noises like talking to hunting friends on your walkie-talkie. Nothing, and I mean nothing, can hurt you more than talking on a radio while deer hunting. The only thing worse is falling asleep on stand. Radios and cell phones should only be used to call for help. Keep the radio on, but on the lowest possible volume. Tell your hunting companions to call you only in an emergency, when they need help dragging a deer, or when they're looking for a buck they just shot. If they want to discuss anything else, make sure they know to wait until you're all back at camp. You're in the woods to hunt deer, not chitchat.

Make the following nine-point pact with yourself before every hunt. It may sound corny, but it really works.

1. I am a good deer hunter.
2. I am confident that I make sound decisions about the hunting strategies I use.
3. I know my quarry's strengths and weaknesses.
4. From this moment on, when I think about deer hunting I will do so with confidence and a positive attitude.
5. When I am in the field, I will totally concentrate on the hunt.
6. I promise I will not let any other matter interfere with my thoughts when I am deer hunting.
7. I will maintain a positive and confident attitude even when I don't see deer during a hunt.
8. I will trust my judgment about the location and tactics I have chosen to use.
9. I am as good a deer hunter as anyone else, and I will hunt that way.

TROPHY HUNTING

If you want to elevate your hunting to the next level by taking larger-racked bucks, follow this simple advice: Learn to be patient and learn to pass up small bucks. I firmly believe that trophy judgment is a personal matter and that any buck you shoot should be treated like a trophy. But if you're committed to bringing home a mature buck, you must also commit to letting younger bucks walk by.

I have heard many hunters describe themselves as trophy hunters, only to see them kill two-year-old bucks. Their excuse for not holding out for a mature buck is almost always the same; they didn't want to get skunked for the season. A hunter who really wants to take bigger bucks must risk going home empty-handed at the end of the season.

To make this new mindset easier to stick with, start small. If you've taken a lot of spikes and four- and six-point bucks in your hunting life, force yourself to pass on any buck with less than eight points. After you've taken a couple of eight-points with antlers twelve to fourteen inches wide, set the bar higher by taking only eight-points with antlers at least sixteen to eighteen inches wide. Once you've bagged a couple of those, commit to taking bucks with eight- or ten-point racks that also have mass and long beams.

Before long, you'll actually start to feel good about letting immature bucks pass by unmolested. You'll have strengthened your resolve to take only obviously mature deer with trophy-class antlers. This is when you become a real trophy hunter.

Trophy-caliber whitetails vary by geographic region due to genetics, food, cover, and so on. A mature trophy buck in your area may mean a sixteen-inch-wide, eight-point buck that scores 120 to 125 B&C points. In other areas, it may mean letting a 140-class buck walk by. And in certain areas of the U.S. and Canada, it may mean watching a 150-class buck saunter away.

This type of hunting isn't easy to do. It's difficult for any hunter to let a solid buck go when it might mean not tagging a deer that season. And it's perfectly fine to decide to take nothing but eight-point bucks or better no matter what they score. Don't let anyone tell you otherwise.

I haven't taken a buck on my farm in the three years I've owned it because we have a Quality Deer Management (QDM) policy. I've had plenty of shot opportunities at racked bucks, but I want to let the smaller bucks mature and become more than just six- and eight-point bucks. It's a personal choice.

But sometimes the aesthetics of a hunt are such that the taking of a lesser buck outweighs the commitment you make to only harvesting a larger, more mature buck. Let your conscience be your guide. If the buck you're looking at makes your heart beat out of your chest, then shoot it. Just don't spend the rest of the year complaining that you never get to see big bucks. The only way you'll ever consistently bag big bucks is to leave the rest alone.

Good luck in the deer woods this season, and remember that you're as good a deer hunter as anyone else. You just have to believe in yourself.

Index

Blat caller
  photo, 91
Bleat, 90, 92, 95, 119–134. *See also*
    specific type
  vs. blat, 95
  doe, 90
  fawn, 120–123
  fawns, 119
  springtime, 95
Blind
  use of, 36
Blood
  amount vs. size, 82
  color, 59
  loss, 62–63
  signs, 69
  trail, 61, 65
    abdominal wounds, 77
    arterial wounds, 79
    broadheads vs. bullets, 82
    heart shot, 76
    intestinal wound, 78
    misconceptions, 62
    stomach wound, 78
Blood, Hal, 5, 29–30
  photo, 6, 30
Blowdowns
  photo, 107
  tracking sign, 33–34
Body, 29–30
Body language, 72
  used to determine wound type,
    73–85
Boggs, Wade, 11
  photo, 144
Boone and Crockett (B&C), 210
Bouckhout, L.W., 235
Bowhunters, 156
Breeding cycle, 151
  elements, 155
  and extreme weather patterns,
    169–170
  late, late phase, 169–170
  length, 189
  and moon phases, 185–190
  North vs. South, 189
  and photoperiodism, 153–156,
    186–188
  and population, 190

post rut, 166–169
pre-rut, 156–162
primary rut, 162–166
stages, 156
and weather, 169–170, 190
Breeding season, 150–174
Brisket shot
  hair identification, 83
Brush
  tracking sign, 33
Buck
  back trail, 33
  vs. doe, 39–45
  largest whitetail recorded, 213–214
  pecking order, 164
  photo, 9, 12, 14, 27, 31, 34, 38, 42,
    52, 54, 61, 66, 98, 100, 109,
    126, 136, 152, 176, 184, 196,
    208, 223
  bedded down, 68
  eating, 230
  from Montana, 164
  8 point, 90, 187
  9 point, 145
  10 point, 124, 129, 144, 189
  12-point, 19
  14 point, 212
  16 point, 134
  tarsal glands, 234
  vocalizing, 93
  physical characteristics *vs.* age, 43
  rub routines, 204
  trolling, 198–202
Bucks
  wounded
    dense cover, 67
    uphill *vs.* downhill, 68–70
Burp grunt, 139, 141
Burp-o-matic grunt, 139
Butski, Paul, 140

C
Cadences, 95
Calendar dates
  and rut, 187
Calling DVD, 122
Calls, 22, 80, 85–146, 240. *See also*
    specific type
  create natural display, 105

Wind *(continued)*
  components, 176–177
  currents, 178
  direction, 177
  reading, 175–184
Windicator
  photo, 182
Wounded bucks
  dense cover, 67
  uphill *vs.* downhill, 68–70

Wounded deer, 57–72
  behavior, 64–71
  hair, 59
  reactions, 73
  seeking water, 70–71
    photo, 71
  uphill race, 70
Wounds
  to primary arteries, 79
  types, 59, 73